The Neuroscience behind the Enneagram

Adelaida Harrison

The Neuroscience behind the Enneagram

How changing yourself… changes everything

Mexico

The Neuroscience behind the Enneagram
How changing yourself…. changes everything

Original title: *Transforma tu vida con el Eneagrama*

1rst edition: December 2019

Copyright © 2019 by Adelaida Harrison Lafuente
© 2019 by Grupo Capdevan SC
CDMX, México
55.6845.6718
info@9egos.com
www.9egos.com

www.eneagramaconocete.com

Translation: Adelaida Harrison
Editing: Dena Benatan
Page Layout: Quinta del Agua Ediciones
Cover Design: Isabel Barbachano

ISBN 978-607-98683-0-7

Contents

Chapter 4

Chapter 5

Chapter 6

Chapter 7

Chapter 8

*Your task is not to find love, but to find
the barriers you have built up against
it.*

RUMI

Acknowledgements

To the Enneagram and to all the people that, thanks to it, I have known around the world and that today are my friends and have left a deep impression on me.

To my students who believed in me and enriched my life with their presence and their experiences.

To Ángeles Lafuente, who helped me structure, format and correct the book, Roberto Pérez who reviewed this material and Fátima Fernández who gave me the prologue of this work.

Andrea Vargas, my first teacher, partner and great friend, who could see in me great potential when I could not.

To Ginger Lapid-Bogda, who in addition to sharing her knowledge with me, teaching me to look for evidence and sticking to the process; helped me achieve very deep transformations in each certification.

To my mother, who taught me that people do not love you as you need, but as they can. To my brothers, because the family is the first emotional school.

To Alexis, Nicole and René, who inspired me to be a better person and helped me to see that education is not about training or restricting, but discovering, caring for and developing the great treasure that they bring in essence from birth. To Jos and Almudena, since they have taught me what unconditional love means. To Jose Ignacio, for loving my treasures and being so supportive to our family.

To René, who helped me to find within me resources that I never imagined, as well as to develop all the tools that I have today.

To God, because the more I learn, the more I marvel of the possibilities we have been given as human beings if we open to His action.

Clarification: I apologize if at any time I involuntarily omitted to give credit to someone for the information received during all these years of trainings and conferences, where I have also received invaluable knowledge.

Introduction

"Instead of living life, life lives us"

Dear reader, I want to share with you a life-changing tool that has helped me and the thousands of people whom we have taught in workshops, companies and through our radio show.

Fifteen years ago, a friend invited me to participate in a workshop, and my answer was: "No thanks, I am a Catholic". "Enneagram" sounded esoteric, and I hesitated a long time before I went, so I perfectly understand the resistance of many people towards it. This is one of the issues that motivated me to write this book. How can a tool that has nothing to do with religion, astrology or numerology be so misunderstood? The answer, I believe, is the lack of preparation of those who teach it, as well as the ignorance of those who judge without taking a closer look at it. So, my first advice to you is don't believe anything you will read here just because I say it; take a look at yourself and put everything I say to the test, and, if it makes sense to you, enjoy the new life that awaits you. My second piece of advice is to learn something new and interesting every day to keep your brain in shape. Listen, analyze and learn from everything that happens to you.

But going back to the matter at hand, I finally took the course and my life changed. A whole new way of looking at life opened up before me, and I even understood my religion better, even though I had always had the need to validate it from a scientific perspective. I managed to do this with my Master's degree in Educational Neurocognition: I was able to make sense out of certain matters I had noticed from the start. I noticed that as soon as I found out people's Enneatype, I ceased to be annoyed by their reactions, and, being aware of this, I could empathize more with them. It is amazing how, thanks to the

Enneagram, radical changes in human behavior are brought about. This happens by changing our perception of what goes on around us. I see how, when one becomes acquainted with it, tolerance and inclusion arise naturally. It is a tool that lets peace and understanding blossom among human beings.

I have trained with a lot of Enneagram teachers, attended conferences, interviewed all the teachers who wanted to share their knowledge with us, and I have bought every Enneagram-related book I have found. It has been an amazing journey of self-discovery. I have shed tears, enjoyed laughter and made great friends across the globe. This book is the result of everything I have learned throughout these years.

My goal is not to create another theory of the Enneagram, but to share the valuable knowledge of every teacher I have had the chance to meet during these fifteen years. I will share with you the concepts that helped me understand this beautiful tool, as well as how it works.

I have looked at the Enneagram from the perspective of new neuroscientific theories to find the foundations that help explain why it is such a powerful tool. I have tried to establish a relation between the Enneagram and the different psychological theories reviewed here, as well as to explain to you its main theories as I understand them. To me, it is evident that there is a close relationship between the Enneagram and the cognitive neurosciences, even though there is still much research to be done. If you are interested in delving into a certain theory, you will find all references at the end of the book, or you can also contact me at info@eneagramaconocete.com and I will be happy to guide you.

You will also see that I've included a QR code in some places. These will take you to videos that help explain the neuroscientific concepts that I discuss. The videos are short but rich in content, and I highly recommend that you watch them – I believe you'll find that they enhance your experience.

I invite you to enter the world of the Enneagram. However, as I said earlier, do not believe anything I say: experience it, take whatever makes sense to you, and discard what is not useful. Mind you, be careful, because for the thousand-plus students I have trained, there is always a before and an after the Enneagram. I guarantee that the after is always for the best...

"If you want to change the world, change yourself."

GANDHI

The Enneagram

What is the Enneagram?

The Enneagram is a powerful self-knowledge tool that studies people and how they relate to others. It reveals in a practical, profound and simple way, nine types of personality or ego: nine different ways to look at life, to think, to feel and to react. Since they are human traits, we all identify a bit with each of them. However, for each of us, one type stands out from the remaining eight, and that is our basic personality type.

This age-old tool has evolved throughout the centuries and today is used on an individual level, as well as in the workplace, literature, education and spirituality.

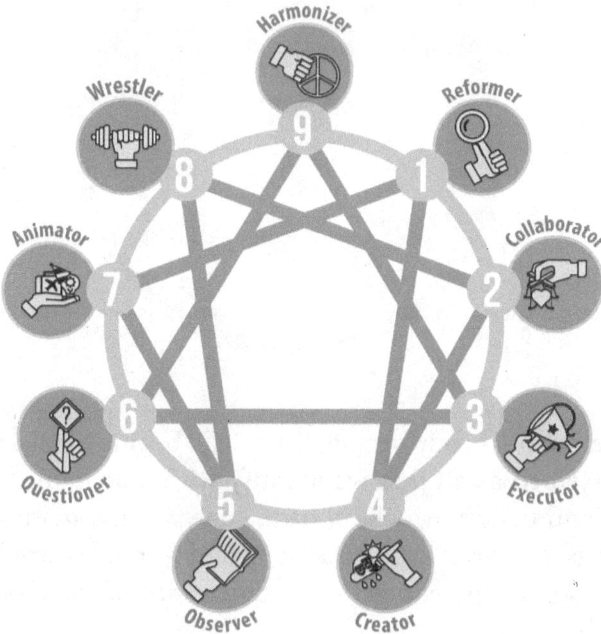

Enneagram is a word of Greek origin. It has two parts:

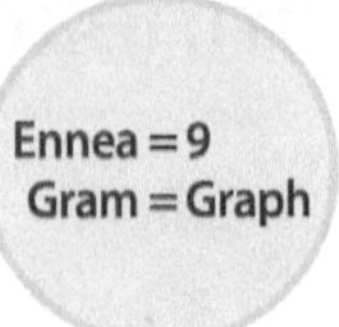

In other words, "graph of nine". It outlines nine different styles of communication, of leadership, of decision-making, of conflict resolution. All of them with virtues and limitations, but none better than the other.

It is symbolized by a circle containing a nine-pointed geometrical shape; the nine points represent the nine personalities and are connected to one another, which allows the system to be rich, dynamic and evolutionary.

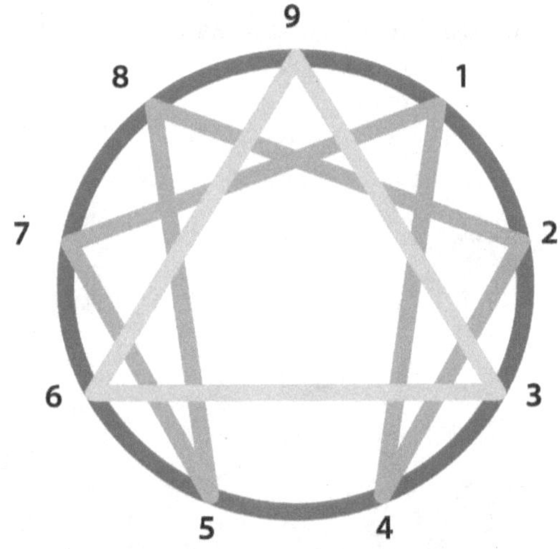

Even before birth, our personality or ego begins to take shape. **Ego** can be described as all that we identify with: our name, nationality, education and beliefs, which, in turn, generate automatic behavioral patterns. It is all stored in our memory, and it molds our identity. According to Buddhism, **ego** is the mistaken idea of **"self"** as an entity that exists by itself.

In a few words, the Enneagram shows everything the person **does but is not**. It describes the attitudes or behaviors we repeat automatically, and that, when we become aware of them, allow us to respond better to situations in our lives. The ego controls and rules our life but it is not our enemy, and it cannot be destroyed, because we created it as a survival mechanism. So, we must understand it as such and learn to give it new meaning. That is, we must learn to use the ego as it is, our servant; this will allow us to retake control of our life. Therefore, the task at hand is to find out what strategy we automatically use so we can take advantage of it. In order to do this, we must learn to *disidentify* from the ego, so we can recognize it as a strategic mask that allows us to survive but does not define us. If we put it in the right place, we will be freer, and therefore happier.

The nine styles of the ego

The Enneagram presents nine different Enneatypes or personalities that I will briefly talk about, and that we will go through in depth in the last chapter of this book.

ONE: The Reformer

Idealist, ethical, structured, thorough

They live by their moral principles and their ideals. They have a very clear idea of what is right and what is wrong. They seek to improve the world and they have very high goals. Integrity, honesty, truth and justice are very important to them. They can be very critical, and they have an internal judge that watches over them constantly.

TWO: The Collaborator

Obliging, attentive, compassionate, generous

They easily recognize needs in others, and they feel proud of lacking needs themselves. They like giving more than receiving. They are warm, good confidants and they are generous with their time. They seek to be loved, needed and indispensable to other people. They may become manipulative in order to reach their goals.

THREE: The Executor

Competent, self-confident, successful, ambitious

They focus their energy on reaching their goals and they are very skilled at adapting to any situation. They seek to earn admiration and prestige. They are always in a hurry; slow people get on their nerves. They see themselves as winners, and they give a lot of importance to this image, as well as to the opinions of others. They may be workaholics as well as highly competitive.

FOUR: The Creator

Authentic, romantic, original, intense

They want everything they do to be original. They are very good at expressing what other people cannot. They seek the intensity of life and to be different from others. They dream and fantasize about romantic moments. Their feelings are deeper than anyone else's. They either suffer a lot or enjoy a lot, and they may have sudden mood changes. They always have the feeling that there is something missing.

FIVE: The Observer

Independent, analytical, withdrawn, inquisitive

They focus deeply on what they like and may neglect other things. They tend to live in their heads and seek to understand the world around them. They may have a hard time with physical work and are not very good at expressing their emotions. They keep an emotional distance from others, and may come across as cold and insensitive.

SIX: The Questioner

Responsible, reliable, committed, ambivalent

Certainty is most important to them. They like things to be clear and to know where they stand. They hesitate a lot before making a decision. They are always on the lookout for danger, for what may go wrong as well as for the intentions of others so they are not taken by surprise. They are skeptical and questioning, with inquisitive and watchful minds. When they feel anxious, their mind wanders to the worst possible scenario. They are either very loyal to authority or they rebel completely against it.

SEVEN: The Animator

Hyperactive, dreamy, flexible, fun

They always look for the opportunities and resources of life. They like freedom and believe that opportunities will not be there forever, so they have to grab them while they last. They constantly seek new and stimulating experiences and are innovative, although they might have a hard time finishing what they start. They may not be very committed, and they are easily distracted.

EIGHT: The Wrestler

Natural leader, direct, decided, assertive

Generous and protective, they are energetic and enthusiastic towards life and work. They inspire others to follow and trust them. They think big. They like control and power. They enjoy confrontation and difficult challenges where they can test themselves. They hate weakness and suffering, which is why they repress anyone who shows these things. Their word is the law, which is why they easily break the rules.

NINE: The Harmonizer

Calm, conciliatory, adaptable, easy-going

They seek to keep inner and outer peace. They avoid conflict and judgment and are impartial most of the time. They simplify their problems and minimize anything that threatens their peace. Harmony is so important to them that they may take on the opinions and interests of others just to keep the peace. Routines and habits provide them with a sense of certainty, though they usually leave important tasks for later.

The Enneagram makes an important distinction between **personality** and **essence**.

Personality can be thought of as a combination of traits used unconsciously by the individual throughout their life. These traits respond to the need of the individual to belong and to guarantee that they will be cared for by their protective figures during childhood. In other words, these traits make up their basic survival strategy.

Naturally, we exaggerate certain desirable features of our own in order to be accepted, while we wear the mask of our personality to conceal our not-so-desirable features, putting them away in our unconscious memory. The result is a maneuver that, since it is used all the time, we forget is only a survival strategy, though it determines the way we look at the world for the rest of our lives. The Enneagram sheds light on those automatic behaviors and, once we understand they are only strategies, we can choose whether we keep on using them or not.

On the other hand, essence is the spiritual part, the **potential me** that lies within every human being: their true nature. Ideally, there would be a balance between personality and essence, because they are both part of the human being.

Let us assume that personality is a horse and essence the rider. Now, if we had no idea we were riding a horse, it would take us wherever it wanted. However, if we realize the horse might obey us and we learn to guide it, then it will take us where we decide to go. This simple fact gives us back power over our life, and it yanks us from the state of helplessness and depression that makes us think life and its circumstances make the decisions for us.

The power to decide

A good way to start to get to know ourselves is to analyze what percentage of our time we make our own decisions in life and what percentage life decides for us.

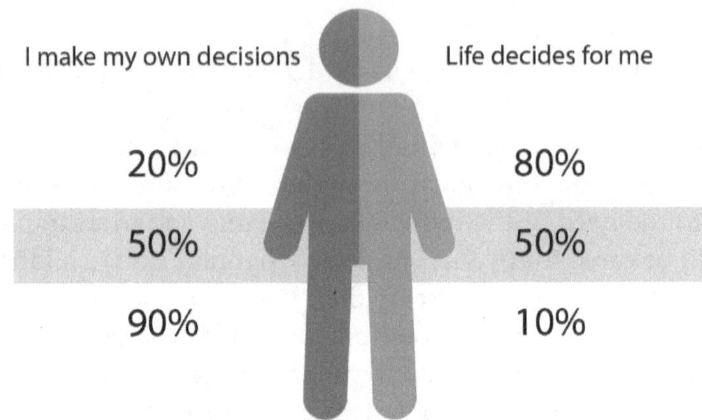

Let us do an exercise to measure our autonomy level. Every answer is valid and personal. Start by writing down your percentages:

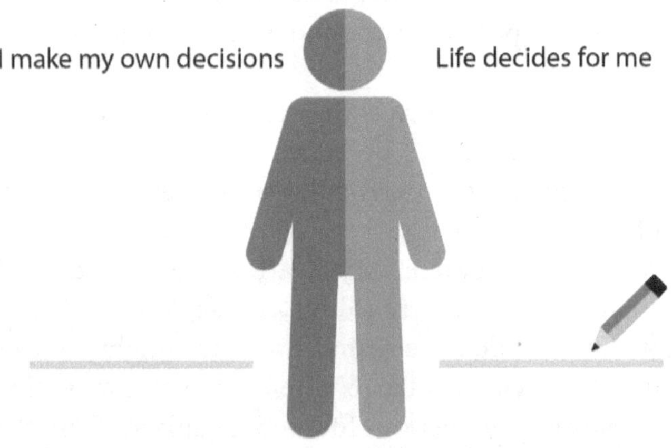

Now, I want you to think of a certain situation where life decides for you. Do not think of something extreme, like death or disease. Here are some recurring situations examples:

- *I begin my day with certain plans, but if my husband calls me and says he left something very important behind, I put my activities on hold and I take it to him.*
- *Since I became a mom, I devote myself to my children, and I cannot do what want to do.*
- *I have to provide for my family, so I cannot quit the job I dislike so much.*

If we look at these statements (and I am sure yours will be very similar), we realize they all stem from the ego mind, or survival mindset. We only pay attention to the activities we cannot do because we have to do other things, but we do not realize that we are also choosing to do what we are doing, giving up on our previous plans… So, we **are** choosing.

Once we realize that, we regain power over our life. This is what true freedom means: knowing we always have another choice and knowing that even the way we react to what happens to us is our decision.

"I was one of those moms who postponed themselves without anyone asking me to do so, until I found myself at 45 with fibromyalgia,(chronic pain) feeling lonely, empty and miserable, despite having a seemingly loving marriage and a perfect family. The problem was that I did not feel loved and, because of this, I could not enjoy my perfect life because it was not mine; it belonged to the person I had made up to be needed and loved. It was really hard for me to admit that I was the only one responsible and that no one but me could change my life. This is what the Enneagram gave me: it gave me back the person I forgot I was. The strategy I used as a child was to see others rather than myself in order to survive, and now I see that no one asked me to do it, it simply happened because I drew the conclusion that it was the best thing to do. I did this with the analytical ability of a child whose brain was not fully developed. One I realized how I nullified myself and how I expected a hidden payback, I began to see other options in life.

> *Naturally, the process of accepting myself with both my sides, good and bad, was painful, because it is not convenient for the family system for someone to move, because you start to confront everyone around you. Then you start to hear remarks like: 'Of course, since you learned the Enneagram you have changed a lot.' 'You are so selfish.' 'I liked you better before.'*
>
> *What I can tell you is that I would do it all again. I would go through all the pain I went through one more time, because I found a much better human being, one who is more complete and satisfied with life. Every change implies some pain, but you stop suffering at the end! So, I can tell you that it is worth the price. The only thing I would do different is that I would not have waited until I was 45, I would have started at 15."*
>
> LUISA (Enneatype Two)

Our society would be different if we all had this tool right from the start. Bullying would stop and social exclusions would cease to exist. Diversity would be encouraged, since, knowing ourselves to be unique and incomparable, we would be committed to achieving our full potential, because no one else can do what we were born to do. We do not need to do new things, we only need to be aware of the patterns we repeat automatically in order to stop repeating them and, in this way, let the potential within us flourish. Parents would only need to recognize their children's abilities and help them with their development.

We came into this world with the necessary kit for completeness, prosperity and happiness… It is just that we do not know it yet, and we try to develop skills we do not have instead of becoming aware of those we naturally do have, in order to nurture them and base our self-esteem on them, instead of on material possessions. Our beliefs determine our reality, and there are many neuroscientific facts that support this. The secret is not locking ourselves up in a room and declaring we want to achieve something. Rather, it is about aligning our mind, body and heart to decide, from our essence, what we really want. Calibrating our attention system to detect opportunities and focus our energy on working in a disciplined way in order to grab them. When we boycott ourselves through our ego, we are only able to see obstacles. Therefore, our brain will provide a hundred reasons why we should not move, plus the hundred reasons others will give us to justify their staying in their own comfort zones.[1]

QR video: Understand the comfort zone

https://youtu.be/HhFxQlDPjaY

Neuroscience, and, more specifically, the Portuguese neuroscientist Antonio Damásio, explains that our actions are motivated by our emotions (the word emotion comes from the Latin *emotio*, which means "putting into action"). The limbic system is the one that triggers automatic behaviors through the short, or reptilian, response system. We also know that all input our brain receives is compared to memories stored in the thalamus… And that our emotions will be determined by our beliefs. The human being lives trying to modify his actions, when what should be changing are his beliefs. That is precisely what the Enneagram does.

Emotion-thought-feeling-action process

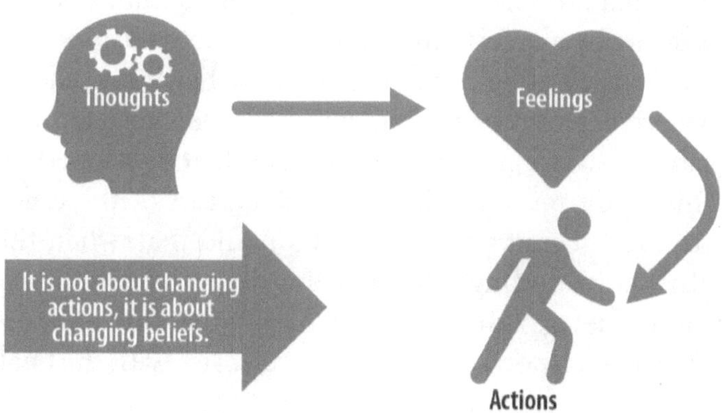

---

[1] https://youtu.be/40mbsKBSWwY

Neuroscience provides theoretical elements that help support the Enneagram. Now I will describe some facts that have been proven by recognized scientists and that explain why the Enneagram changes the worldview of the human being so deeply. They serve as a foundation to the theory that maintains that the ego or Enneatype is a survival mechanism with a biological origin that arises as a response to each person's childhood conditions. Moreover, it deeply transforms brain structures.

Personality: Nature or nurture?

My students constantly ask me this question: Are we born with our personality, or do we develop it? Experts' opinions are extremely divided regarding this subject. Scientific journalist Anne Murphy's[2] "fetal origins hypothesis" may serve as a guide to answer it.

From the biological point of view, nature needs to guarantee the survival of the species, ensuring that the individual's genes are passed on to the next generation. Nature's job is to keep the individuals on this planet to achieve its objective. This means that the conditions in which life is present do not matter that much, as long as they guarantee the existence of offspring. An example of this are children who are born in conditions of extreme poverty in Africa, who have an adapted metabolism that is capable of surviving with the minimal amount of nutrients. Murphy suggests the idea that the fetus begins to adapt to its environment even before being born. In her book, she mentions a study where a group of people who had been gestated during the "Dutch famine"[3] were monitored, and who had developed obesity as adults. This study revealed that the metabolism of these adults had adapted to food scarcity during gestation and that, when the conditions of their surroundings changed, they had become obese.

Moreover, she explains that the baby identifies and prefers its mother's voice to any other, and that it even cries with the characteris-

---

[2] *Origins, How the Nine Months Before Birth Shape the Rest of Our Lives*
[3] The Dutch Famine took place in the Netherlands during the winter of 1944-45, near the end of World War II.

tic intonation of its language. She also states that it prefers the smells and flavors of the food its mother ingested during gestation, because it deems them safe to eat.

Murphy explains that everything experienced in the womb can condition health, well-being and abilities all the way to adulthood. She mentions that it is perhaps in the womb where the most significant learning takes place for the human being. She says, supported by several case studies, that gestation crucially affects the quality of life of the human being.

This theory could reconcile the two existing positions regarding personality formation among the Enneagram theorists. Because, even though the Enneatype is a biological adaptation that is a result of certain circumstances, it is also possible that Enneatype is determined before birth.

The origins of discrimination

Another thing working for the survival of human beings is keeping away from the unknown. For the brain, anything different to what it is used to falls into the category of suspicious or dangerous. Therefore, it will naturally keep us away from it. The origin of many types of discrimination may well be here. Our first response in the face of uncertainty is stress, which prepares the body for fight or flight. American psychologist Daniel Goleman points out that, "it is no wonder that those small primates (*homo sapiens*) who were alerted before the smallest threat were the only ones whose descendants were able to survive and write books about it".[4]

Thus, any new thing might constitute a potential threat to the brain, so it must be explored. Even though attention generates stress, stress, in turn, sharpens the process of attention. It is evident that, if we are so concerned with keeping our genes safe, a proper diet will not be the priority, nor will establishing healthy bonds with anyone, even less looking to learn from such a situation.

---

[4] Goleman, D. (2014), *El punto ciego (Blind Spot), Me gusta leer*, p. 61.

Nowadays, unlike our primate ancestors, our life is not usually in any real danger, yet we still operate under the premise that different means dangerous. Violence and aggression are biological response mechanisms when we believe that we are at a disadvantage in the face of an unknown situation. This could be a biological explanation for the levels of violence currently being experienced. Human beings, like all animals, only attack when they feel at a disadvantage. Therefore, the only way to end violence is to transform our perception of feeling threatened. That is why the Enneagram brings about such significant transformations, because it modifies the system of beliefs regarding difference, and enables the updating of perception mechanisms. By recognizing there are nine valid ways to look at life, the brain ceases to perceive what is different as dangerous, because it realizes that taking into account all nine perspectives may hugely increase the probabilities of survival.

Personality as a survival strategy

Each personality develops different ways to deal with stressful situations when it cannot do it properly. Stress makes us vigilant and triggers a series of physiological reactions. Our brain releases cortisol and prepares us to flee from the predator or to fight and defend ourselves. Many human beings live in a state of stress 24/7. However, this biological mechanism was designed to last only for short periods of time, because while we are on the alert, all non-vital functions are suspended. When faced with high and prolonged levels of stress, our brain will look for ways to reduce it to tolerable levels, despite not being healthy. This means that if our brain does not have sufficient elements to solve a problem in reality, it will do so with its imagination.

When someone who promised to call us does not, our mind starts suggesting possible reasons why that person has not called us, and in less than an hour we have already made up a story and convinced ourselves that it is real in order to stop worrying. This process takes us out of the alert-stress cycle to send us directly to action or defense. For example, we get upset because we already know they did not call us because they did not care about their commitment to us, to which we add motives: "*They do not care about me, they are drunk for sure, they went shopping with their friends and forgot about me*", and so on. But we seldom wait for news before; making judgments or jumping to conclusions.

This strategy, known as coping, which was developed to aid our survival, may limit our lives in unfathomable ways. American writer and lecturer[5] Lou Tice talks about a creative unconscious, which provides us with simple solutions to tackle stress and tension. For example, when faced with the dilemma of undertaking a new project, we feel stress, and our creative unconscious will help us solve it by taking us towards a place with more energy. If we are afraid to do it, our creative unconscious will give us a hundred reasons or motives why we should not do it. However, if we really want to go for it, then it will provide a hundred ways to accomplish it. It is all based on what motivation we may or may not have.

A study on the decision-making process of the brain and thoughts, conducted at the Washington University in St. Louis[6], proved that the parts of the brain which activate when imagining the future or recalling the past are the same, despite there being eight brain regions more involved when imagining the future. This research suggests that our decisions and our actions are based on our past experiences. The Enneagram helps discover the story our brain has told us throughout our life, so we can modify it and have a greater understanding of reality. This will give us a better chance to respond properly to our current situation, instead of reacting from our own personal history.

The ego sees what it wants to see

As we have already seen, what we call reality is far from being "The Reality", because our beliefs determine the way we look at the world.

---

[5] Tice, L. (2005), *Smart Talk For Achieving Your Potential*, Pacific Institute Publishing.

[6] Karl K. Szpunar and Jason M. Watson at the Washington University in St. Louis, (2007), using a functional nuclear magnetic resonance (fNMR).

This skill is known as selective attention. There are many tests that reveal how our brain tricks us constantly.[7]

QR video: Selective attention test

https://youtu.be/IGQmdoK_ZfY

The brain cannot process every single stimulus around it because we would go crazy. Therefore, stimuli are filtered according to one priority: Survival! Selective attention is the result of several brain processes, but it basically means focusing on what the brain considers important to ensure survival and thus guaranteeing that our genes remain a part of the genetic pool of humanity.

Paying attention to one thing means we do not pay attention to information that is not useful at the time. For example, when we read something written on a striped notebook, we pay attention to the words, not the stripes. However, if someone asks us what color the stripes are, then our brain will focus on the stripes and not on the words.

Each Enneatype pays attention to what they consider useful for their survival. Knowing the story our ego tells us will help us change our deepest beliefs and remodel our frames of reference. Having a less distorted perception of our environment allows us to make better decisions. The brain increases its ability to perceive by transforming attentional structures.

The ego would rather be right than happy

Faced with the need to solve every situation quickly and with the least amount of energy possible, the brain designed a fast decision-making system which is based on looking for references to similar past situations in order to act in ways that have previously proved successful.

---

[7] Selective attention test link: https://youtu.be/IGQmdoK_ZfY

In other words, in the face of any unknown situation, it looks for a similar situation where action was taken successfully and acts according to it. To accomplish this, classifying situations becomes indispensable for survival. Therefore, the brain cannot go around asking itself whether its reference points are valid or not. It just starts from a basis that it considers reliable and takes it from there until circumstances prove otherwise.

To the human brain, making a wrong decision may prove fatal. For example, mistaking a poisonous snake for a tree branch could prove fatal. Despite the fact that, nowadays, our physical safety is not usually in such danger, making mistakes still causes us problems. For example, if a teacher asked us a question and we did not know the answer, we were in danger. So, our brain learned that it **has to be right** in order to survive. That is why, for the primitive brain, people who think differently challenge our frame of reference and question our ability to face life. Since they represent a reality that we do not know how to handle, we immediately try to convince them that our point of view is right.

The problem with this type of education, which is still common today, is that we think we will no longer be able to acquire the abilities we did not develop. Therefore, every time we find ourselves in a situation where others do not share our reality, our brain evaluates our abilities as a person. Since we already consider ourselves a "finished product", we have no option but to defend with tooth and nail our truth and impose it on the rest of the world. American psychologist Carol Dweck[8] called this type of mindset "Fixed Mindset". It is based on the idea and belief that the brain cannot learn anything new.

QR video: Fixed mindset vs growth mindset

https://youtu.be/KUWn_TJTrnU

---

[8] Dweck, Carol (2016), *Mindset: The New Psychology of Success,* Random House.

The latest studies on the subject have shown that we cannot determine whether people have one mindset or another. The Enneagram suggests that there are nine different ways to look at life, which helps people relax their mindset and transform it into what Dweck calls a "Learning Mindset". By introducing the idea that taking into account all nine points of view that the Enneagram suggests will give us a wider perspective of reality, we radically increase our chances of survival. Learning mechanisms will get going on their own, because the old brain will be thirsty for new experiences and, therefore, open to other points of view.

The ego mindset

The attention system of a person is calibrated according to their stress level. According to the Enneagram, there are two types of mindsets that coexist within us:

1. Ego mindset

In the fixed or **ego** mindset, we can say we are in **survival mode**, because Enneatypes are only able to perceive danger and potential threats. In other words, when the brain is busy helping us survive, it does not care about emotional fatigue nor general well-being; it is only worried about keeping our body, or rather our genes, safe, so they can be passed on to the next generation. Cortisol levels are at the highest, and digestion processes will be disrupted while we are in survival mode, which, as we have already seen, should only last a few minutes, while we flee or face the predator.

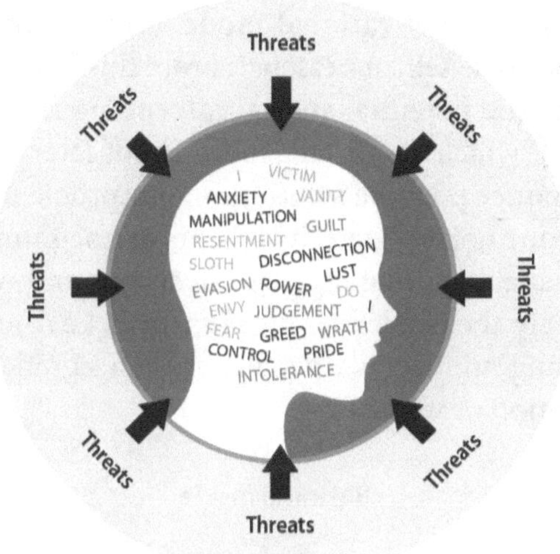

While this mindset is active, the brain will always be busy looking out for danger and potential predators around us. American cellular biologist Bruce Lipton[9] says in an interview called "Why we get sick"[10] that if we are not growing, we are dying, because this state consumes and degrades the organism if it lasts too long. He has conducted several studies on the effect the environment has on cellular development and on the organism. He states that our beliefs have an influence on every aspect of our life, even our health.

QR video: Bruce Lipton: Why we get sick?

https://www.youtube.com/watch?v=YZHFg1zo4zA

---

[9] Lipton, B. (2007), *La biología de la creencia (The Biology of Beilief)*, 1ª ed. Madrid: Palmira.

[10] Lipton, B. https://www.youtube.com/watch?v=YZHFg1zo4zA

2. Essence mindset

We will call this mindset **rational mode**. It means that we are truly connected to our true self, our essence. From this place, we will be able to develop our true potential and our ascending reticular activating system (ARAS), which I will talk more about later, will be focused on helping us notice possible solutions to our problems. Even though this should be our normal state, it is the most uncommon. In rational mode we are capable of making good decisions and we can respond instead of react to the challenges life puts forth. Learning to live more with this learning mindset is what allows for a significant increase in people's perception of well-being.

Rational mode

I have observed that, after changing their beliefs, people are able to reach the goals they had not been able to attain previously and their lives transform radically. When the feeling of being threatened by the environment is reduced, perception filters relax and the brain structure is remodeled. I will go further into this in Chapter 2. This allows for the alignment of the brain's energy with opportunities for expansion, as they are no longer focused on challenges and dangers that may have been valid during childhood, but that, today, are only holding them back.

A dash of Neuroscience

Neuroplasticity is the basis of transformation

Not long ago, the generally held belief was that a human being was born with a particular set of skills and died with them. Neuroscience has shown that a baby's brain is full of possibilities… and that it cannot be genetically determined because there would not be enough DNA to transmit the necessary information to model it. In other words, we are born with millions of neurons more than we need, and they give us the potential to develop the fittest brain structure to survive and adapt to the environment we live in.

The brain is modified throughout our life, not only during childhood; it changes constantly and has the ability to recover and restructure. This transformation is known as "neuroplasticity".[11] This concept is key to understanding why the brain of each Enneatype has a specific structure that can be remodeled to recover its full potential.

The Matthew Effect, a concept used in education, refers to the biblical quote[12] *"For to him who has, will more be given; and from him who has not, even what he has will be taken away"*. That is how the brain works… If it is used, it grows and develops more skills, and if it is not, its neuronal connections decrease by the day. That is why it is so important to read, because it increases our intellectual capacity. People who do not read are less able to learn and reason. The more flexible our mindset is and the greater interest we have in listening to other points of view, the greater our consciousness and the possibilities to have a better life will be.

---

[11] http://www.scielo.org.co/pdf/cesm/v28n1/v28n1a10.pdf
[12] MT 13:12.

If we have already seen that the brain filters and focuses on the stimuli it deems important for survival, we can assume it has the ability to structure itself in order to accomplish an efficient interconnectivity that allows it to support its basic survival strategy. That is why it builds and broadens the highways used for communication between brain areas: to make it easier and more efficient. This process also allows it to disconnect and eliminate useless connections, using mechanisms such as synaptic pruning and hyperconnectivity.

Mechanisms of neuroplasticity

Synaptic pruning

"Synaptic pruning" is like gardening: the brain prunes useless or painful brain connections, and favors the ones that are useful.[13] This inhibition can be either temporary, to focus on a specific task without being distracted by unrelated stimuli, or permanent, when a connection is too painful.

A baby is born with many more synaptic connections than it can use; therefore, its brain lacks specificity. On the other hand, the adult brain has fewer synaptic connections, but it is much more efficient, because its connections are specific to its needs for survival. Mexican psychologist Dr. Feggy Ostrosky, who has a doctorate in biomedicine, says, along with other investigators, that there is a process parallel to synaptic formation that stems from gestation. They reached the conclusion that both processes have the function of achieving an ideal brain structure that ensures survival. They affirm that, *"At the beginning, the overproduction of neurons may give the brain maximum capacity to respond to the environment and form multiple connections. Afterwards, during development, the neurons or synapses that do not receive stimulation are eliminated, which allows for a greater degree of specialization through the refinement of synaptic connections."*[14]

---

[13] https://youtu.be/rxPT78F_ZVE

[14] Ostrosky-Solís F, Gómez-Pérez, Próspero-García O. The development of attention, memory and the inhibitory processes: the chronological relation with the maturation of brain structure and functioning, *Rev Neurol.* 2003;37(6):561-567.

QR video: Understand Synaptic Prunning

https://youtu.be/rxPT78F_ZVE

Neural hyperconnectivity

This is the opposite phenomenon to synaptic pruning. It implies that used connections become deeper and stronger in order to facilitate the passing of information, until an information superhighway is built in the brain to channel the most useful routes. This is done with the purpose of responding quickly and efficiently to life's challenges. Maybe that is why it is so hard to change our habits, because our brain always chooses the easy path, the one with which it is familiar.

Ascending Reticular Activating System (ARAS)

The ARAS is responsible for maintaining the attention focused on the stimuli that are important to each Enneatype. This mechanism works automatically even when we are asleep. But if we are not aware of how it works, we most likely do not know how to calibrate it to help us accomplish our goals.

Here is an example of this natural process: When we want to lose weight, we start a diet; however, the brain does not care about figure or vanity. It simply understands that without food, it dies… and we are "starving" it. What is it going to do? It will focus on every dessert, candy and delicious greasy food around us. We will never notice the slim bodies we wish we had. The reason is that our brain wants us to survive, and to survive, we need to eat! Therefore, our mind will often focus on how hard it is to diet with all those culinary delights around us, drastically decreasing our chances of success. So, it is necessary to outline the diet in a way that our amygdala does not trigger the mechanism of survival and spoil the whole thing. This process is known as recalibrating our Ascending Reticular Activating System (ARAS).

QR video: Reticular Activation System

https://youtu.be/QCnfAzAlhVw

Depending on our mindset, the ARAS will be responsible for detecting threats or potential opportunities. Here are some examples of how our ARAS operates according to our interests. One of them is how mothers who are able to sleep soundly, even if a train passes them by, immediately wake up to the slightest sound uttered by their children; or how when we decide to buy a red car of any given brand, we start seeing red cars of the brand we want everywhere, seemingly by chance. The actual number of red cars on the road is the same; it is just that our ARAS is more aware of them because it considers it to be important to us at that time.

When we have a problem, we think about it all day. But that will never help us solve it. This is called "ruminative thinking"; the brain will never be able to find a way out, because it calibrated the ARAS to pay attention to the problem. Each Enneatype develops selective attention towards certain stimuli, and their ARAS is calibrated to detect them. When we transform the beliefs that uphold personality, the ARAS recalibrates and perception is drastically widened, allowing us to see solutions rather than problems.

Scotoma

This term comes from the Greek *skótos*, which means darkness. It is often used in ophthalmology to describe a black dot on a person's field of vision, but it is also used in psychology to describe things we leave out of our view in order to avoid suffering.

Each Enneatype has a specific scotoma. It represents the attitudes a person neither perceives nor is aware of, but that affect their relationships. It is known as our *shadow*. Our brain removes it from our conscious radar to prevent us from feeling uncomfortable; however, it is the very thing that annoys us the most.

When the Enneagram gives rise to the awareness of scotomas and the problems they cause, the brain modifies and updates its strategies so they are useful for survival. That is why the use of this tool brings about deep transformations and huge increases in productivity.

The story our ego told us

It is evident that there is a close relationship between the Enneagram and neuroscience, especially neurocognition. The users of this system have significant attitude changes, and some groups have reported an increase of up to 40%[15] on the relative well-being index. The Enneagram brings about deep changes in the way we perceive life. The attentional filter relaxes, and people begin opening up to other options. In other words, they receive stimuli, or a more varied input, that allows them to have a broader view of their life. Thanks to that, they are able to make better decisions and to be more assertive.

"Since I participated in the Enneagram workshop, I get angry and scream less often. I have learned to see alternatives that allow me to solve my problems in a different way. I stopped feeling helpless and now I do not let passion come over me and I enjoy my children more."

Rocío (Enneatype 4)

The Enneagram increases the emotional intelligence of those who learn it and embrace it in their lives. This in itself would be a topic for neuroscientific research, because when the attentional filter relaxes or

---

[15] These results were obtained in a pilot program conducted in cooperation with Proeducación, IAP and with parents from a public school in Mexico City.

broadens, the amygdala ceases to trigger the "Survival Mode" or short response when faced with stimuli, and allows information to be analyzed via the longer way, that is, via the "Rational Mode". This effect is very similar to that of meditation, which is why the Enneagram generates mindfulness.

Many systems of teaching operate based on the premise that each child learns in a different way, yet these ways are not described. Therefore, teachers are expected, in a way, to become circus clowns, trying to find an entertaining manner in which to present information in order to capture the students' attention. In my opinion, all they actually have to take into account is that each personality has a different motivation to learn, but that they all are based on the principle *"If it is not useful for my survival, I do not listen to it, much less learn it."*

The Enneagram describes the motivation of each Enneatype. Like teachers, parents, too, can use the Enneagram to help unlock the potential of each of their children.

It has become generally accepted that learning processes depend to a great extent on the attention we pay, which, in turn, is determined by the existing motivation to acquire the knowledge being shared, yet no one links them to a biological process of survival. Israeli historian Yuval Noah[16] says that the *homo sapien's* ability to gossip allowed us to evolve over every other species of hominids. We need only notice the interest we place on gossip. However, not many of us realize that it has a biological purpose: it warns us of danger. In other words, if the information seems relevant to our survival, we will pay more attention to it.

When a child's basic needs are not properly satisfied, they begin to experience deficiencies that generate deep anxiety, since they are related to the risk of death. As mentioned last chapter, children know they depend on their carers for their survival, and in the first months of their lives they develop strategies that help them guarantee it. The result is a strategy that becomes so over-used, that we forget it is nothing but that, a survival strategy, but which will determine the way we

---

[16] Harari, Yuval Noah (2016), *Sapiens. De animales a dioses (Sapiens. A Brief History of Humankind,* Debate.

see the world for the rest of our life. This gives rise to the basic belief, *"I will be fine if I act in a certain way"*, which will become an order to the brain. Each Enneatype is based on a basic fear of not being how they should be, which is compensated by a particular basic desire, thus giving rise to personality or **ego**.

The beliefs of the ego

Personality	Belief	Basic Fear	Basic Desire and its cognitive distortion
1	I will be fine if I do the right thing.	Fear of being bad or imperfect.	Desire for integrity, which degenerates into critical perfectionism.
2	I will be fine if I am loved by others.	Fear of being unworthy of love.	Desire to be loved, which degenerates into the need to be needed.
3	I will be fine if I am successful.	Fear of being worthless.	Desire to be valuable, which degenerates into a need for success.
4	I will be fine if I am true to myself.	Fear of lacking identity.	Desire to be oneself, which degenerates into self-complacency.
5	I will be fine if I am competent.	Fear of being incompetent.	Desire to be competent, which degenerates into a useless specialization.
6	I will be fine if I am safe.	Fear of lacking support.	Desire for security, which degenerates into a strong attachment to beliefs and a hunt for trust.
7	I will be fine if I am optimistic.	Fear of suffering.	Desire to be happy, which degenerates into an incessant hunt for pleasure.
8	I will be fine if I am strong and in control.	Fear of being vulnerable.	Desire for protection, which degenerates into an incessant and unnecessary struggle.
9	I will be fine if I do not cause trouble.	Fear of losing connection, and of conflict.	Desire to be at peace, which degenerates into stubborn negligence.

Chart based on the messages, fears and desires of each Enneatype according to Riso and Hudson.

CHAPTER 3

Where does the Enneagram come from?

The first serious research about the origins of the Enneagram was conducted by Mexican sociologist Fátima Fernández Christlieb[17], who found in it a wonderful tool of self-knowledge and communication. Being an academic, she decided to undertake the task of doing an exhaustive and documented revision, which cleared up several myths and history.

The Enneagram has endured for centuries as a part of human spiritual philosophy. Today, it is important to connect it to the tools neuroscience provides in order to make the most out of it, in a current and dynamic fashion.

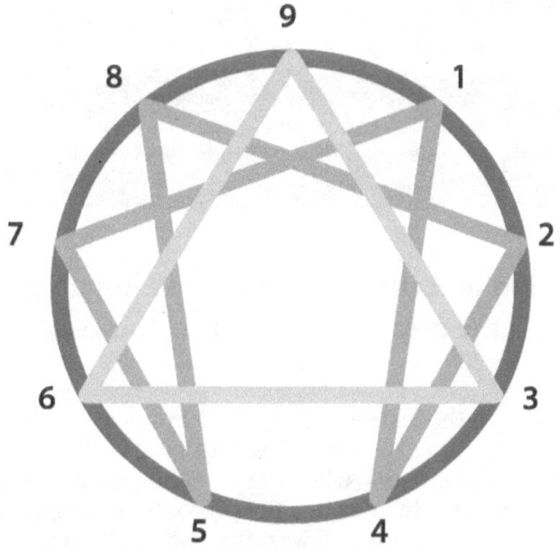

---

[17] "The beginning was clear: the region between the Tigris and the Euphrates would be my entry gate, which also turned out to be an articulating axis that took me from two thousand years before Christ all the way to the 20th century. (...) I found reliable evidence of the Chaldean matrix of the number nine, as well as of the use of the circumference and the desire to attain the absolute from the human corporeality.

The passions of the Enneagram

Each Enneatype or personality is dominated by a certain passion or what is referred to as a capital sin.

Sin, according to its earliest origin, is related to a mistaken or incorrect perception, rather than to a specific action. Aristotle used the word *hamartia* to refer to an error, mistake or sin. In other words, *hamartia* can be translated as "to err" or "to miss the mark". In archery, this concept of sin would make reference to the distance between the target and the place where the arrow fell.

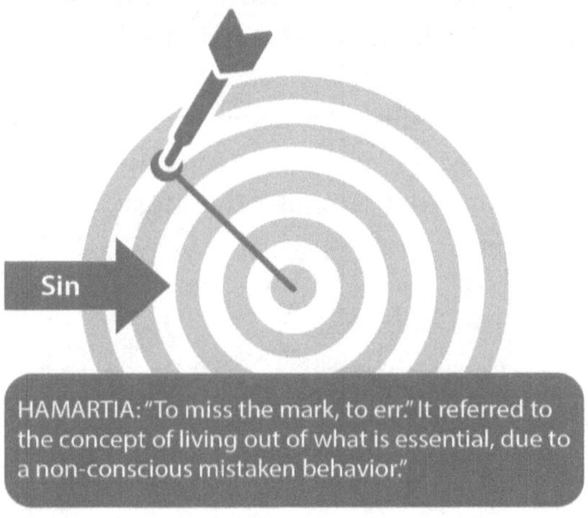

The Enneagram describes passion as the impulse that separates us from our essence; the greater the distance, the greater the separation.

These clearly emerged in the legacy of Evagrius Ponticus. I verified the use of a very similar symbol to the one that is used today, with nine vices and virtues, in the work of Ramon Llull in the 13th century, when the great Sufi Masters explicitly stated their practical morals with great coincidences. The proto-enneagrams made by Athanasius Kircher in the 17th century sprang up. I was surprised by the environment of the Eastern Orthodox churches where Gurdjieff was born, his interest in the Essenes, and his condition of victim after the Armenian Genocide where his father was killed. I managed to understand why so many Jesuit priests made incursions into the Enneagram: it was not because some of them liked the esoteric, or because the symbol seemed like a challenge; they entered this knowledge because their tradition, over four centuries old, led them to organicistic and complex views of the world." [Fernández Christlieb, Fátima (2016), *¿De dónde demonios salió el Enneagrama?*, Ed. Pax, pp. 11-12].

That is what we nowadays know as sin, mistaken actions or responses. There is great richness in that, because it is possible to change our behaviors and to stop sinning. The Enneagram also tells us that fear makes us vigilant to external dangers, and this makes us lose contact with our essence or soul.

When we drift away from our essence, we forget who we are. That is why we start developing strategies that allow us to function in an unfavorable environment. This is how we develop the **ego** or personality.

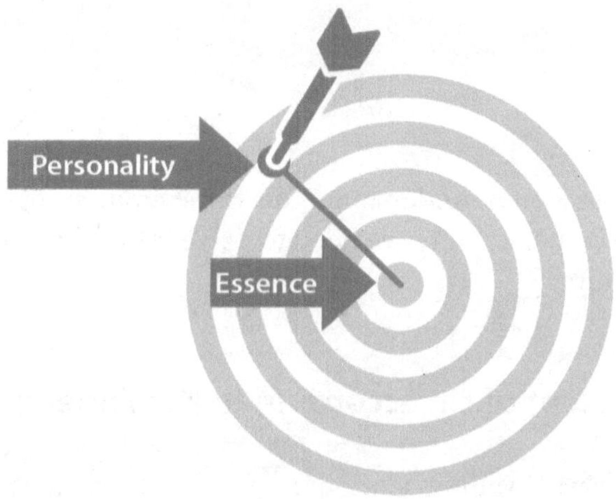

The first person to describe this process of separation through thoughts was Evagrius Ponticus, a 4th century Egyptian monk and one of the so-called Desert Fathers or mystics of early Christianity. German theologist Johannes Quasten presents him as the "founder of monastic mysticism and the most prolific and interesting spiritual author of the Egyptian desert. The Eastern and Western monks studied his writings as classic documents and as manuals of incalculable value".[18]

In the Enneagram, each personality is linked or related to a **capital sin**, which, in its broadest sense, refers to the corrupt state that is brought about by being distanced from God. In current terms, it is the primordial mistake that gives rise to every other sin we commit in life.

---

[18] González, J., Rubio, J. (2013), *Evagrio Póntico, obras espirituales,* Ed. Ciudad Nueva.

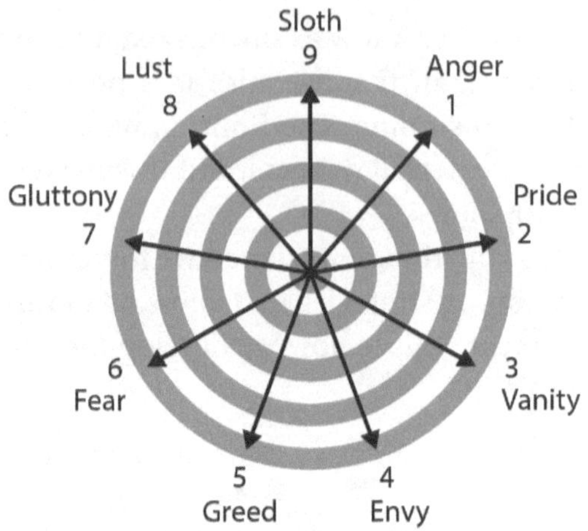

In order to better understand the Enneagram's approach to the passion-driven personality, we need to delve into the ancient meaning of the word **sin**.

Concept of sin according to the Enneagram

The first desert-dwelling Christian mystics from the 4th century, known as the Desert Fathers, believed that thoughts were responsible for human beings' behavior. They divided them into good and bad or sinful thoughts, because they generated a mistaken perception of reality that was toxic for the individual. Origen of Alexandria (185-254), considered one of the three pillars of Christian theology, said that bad thoughts come from the heart[19]. He observed that *"the source and origin of every sin are sinful thoughts"*[20].

Christian theologian and sage Saint Maximus the Confessor advised on the importance of watching thoughts, because the first sins arise in the mind, and the "oversights" of fundamental principles are multiplied. The Fathers and Monks of the Desert called them *"scotosis"*, a state of mind that agrees to mistaken ways of thinking, which are based on van-

---

[19] See *Mt* 15:19.
[20] *Commentary on the Gospel of Matthew*, 21.

ity itself and on the existential lie. All of this brings about certain inner conditions that favor the spread of vice and sin. We will see how this idea reflects on the approach the Enneagram takes on mental fixations.

Evagrius Ponticus also stressed the need to be on the lookout for the appearance of **mistaken ideas**. Evagrius' ideas gave rise to what would later be known as "capital sin"; in this context, the word 'capital' means the head of every other passion. This implies becoming aware of the sin or mistake that generates every other mistake of perception that distances us from the essence[21], which is directly linked to the current goal of the Enneagram. That is why each Enneatype is related to a capital sin as well as to a mental fixation. In other words, it is a toxic thought that generates distorted emotions or passions that trigger incorrect actions in the individual, which the Enneagram describes in an accurate and detailed manner.

Evagrius thought that the soul must face repetitive and toxic thoughts[22] that hover over the mind like "flies on a wound", because they carry confusion and restlessness, and they are a great obstacle when one is looking for God.

The Enneagram describes these toxic thoughts as mental fixations typical to each Enneatype:

1. Perfectionism
2. Adulation
3. Self-deceit
4. Melancholy
5. Isolation
6. Doubt
7. Planning
8. Revenge
9. Indolence

These toxic thoughts or mental fixations produce a base emotion or mood, known in Christianity as capital sin. Mexican theologist

---

[21] God.
[22] *Logismoi.*

Cristina Babatz defines them as *"thoughts that trigger negative and anxiety-filled emotions, which produce chemical changes in our organism and cause stress"*.

Later on, we find an explicit reference to the nine capital sins that the Enneagram sets out. 14th century beatus Ramon Llull makes a list of the nine passions or capital sins in his work *Ars Brevis*, and he includes a figure which is very similar to the current Enneagram:

First printed Enneagram. Llull, R., *Ars Brevis* (1432)

The use of this image was authorized by the Virtual Library of Bibliographic Heritage, Spain.

The letters symbolize the nine passions or capital sins the Enneagram works with:

B. Greed
C. Gluttony
D. Lust
E. Pride

F. Sloth

G. Envy

H. Wrath

I. Falsehood

K. Fickleness

Holy ideas, virtues and fixations

We must also take into account another concept that the Enneagram offers. Contrary to what we refer to as personality, we have the essence, which is the true part of each human being, that which is valuable in them. It is what Saint Teresa, founding nun of the Order of the Discalced Carmelites, called the "Seventh Mansion" (or dwelling place); Saint Augustine, Father and doctor of the Catholic Church, called it "Soul".

The Enneagram mentions that each personality, or Enneatype, possesses, in essence, a special way of looking at undistorted reality. It is a mental attribute, known as the Holy Idea. In modern terms, it is the healthy view of reality that the Being has when individuals are connected to their essence. When this connection is lost, fixation arises, also known as a toxic thought pattern, according to Evagrius. This gives rise to the specific passion of each personality. In other words, thoughts produce an emotion that, in the case of the Sacred Idea, will be the distinct virtue of each personality. In the case of a mental fixation, it will be the belief that generates the related passion or capital sin.

Philosopher Oscar Ichazo[23], the person who transformed the Enneagram into what we know today, is credited with the idea of placing the attributes of each person in the symbol of the Enneagram, giving rise to several different Enneagrams. The most widely spread are the Enneagram of Virtues, the Enneagram of Passions, the Enneagram of Fixations and the Enneagram of Sacred Ideas. Ichazo presented the

---

[23] Oscar Ichazo was born in Bolivia in 1931. He studied philosophy and metaphysics and travelled around the world seeking ancient knowledge. He is the founder of the Arica School. Ichazo's theory of the Enneagram of Personality is part of a wider set of teachings that he calls Protoanalysis, whose goal is attaining the Supreme Good of Enlightenment and Unity with the Divine. He created the concept of Sacred Ideas, which are applicable to all nine types of personality.

idea of passion and virtue as opposing behaviors.

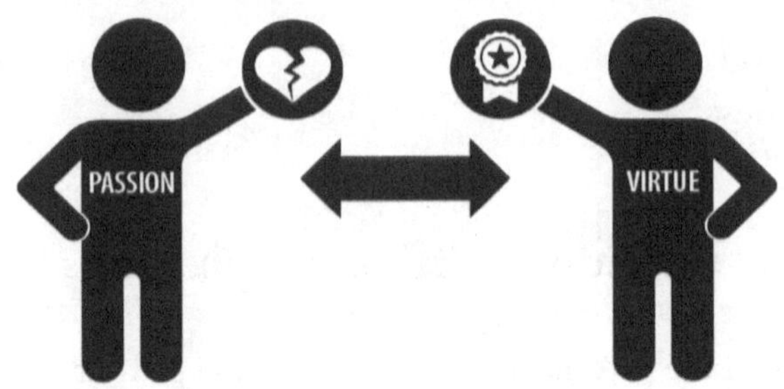

Summary of holy ideas, virtues, fixations and passions

Personality	Holy Idea	Virtue	Fixation	Passion
1	Holy Perfection	Serenity	Resentment	Anger
2	Holy Freedom	Humility	Flattery	Pride
3	Holy Hope	Truthfulness	Vanity	Self-deceit
4	Holy Origin	Equanimity	Melancholy	Envy
5	Holy Omniscience	Non attachment	Stinginess	Avarice
6	Holy Faith	Courage	Cowardice	Fear
7	Holy Plan	Sobriety	Planning	Gluttony
8	Holy Truth	Innocence	Vengeance	Lust
9	Holy Love	Right Action	Indolence	Sloth

Chart based on the Enneagrams created by Oscar Ichazo.

How is personality formed?

Personality according to the Enneagram

The word "personality" has its origin in classical theatre. Greeks used to wear masks to represent different characters. The mask was also useful in helping the actors' voices to be heard better; that is why Romans called it *"per sonare... so that voice sounds better."*

Personality can be defined as something that is not one's own, something that is an add-on as opposed to something essential.

Personality, according to the Enneagram, is a cognitive process that develops in early childhood, through which all the information we receive throughout our life is processed but which responds to the needs of a child that depends on adults to survive.

By becoming aware of this automatic pattern, the individual begins to question whether such a cognitive process is still useful now that he has a fully developed neocortex and has grown so that he no longer depends on his protective figures for his survival.

The Enneagram helps in understanding the nine different attentional filters that define the information relevant for survival through which life is perceived. And through a new learning process, we can design strategies that best adapt to our current situation.

From my point of view, it is not so much the learning style but the attention and motivation systems that define our reality and that are perfectly described by the Enneagram. By relaxing the attentional filters and actualizing basic motivation systems, we can see an increase in the so-called emotional intelligence that enhances all kinds of human relationships.

"My first contact with the Enneagram generated anguish, anger, rejection. I couldn't believe that there was any possible way of being rather than right. I didn't like seeing myself in that mirror, and I preferred to turn the other way, just ignore it, I wasn't ready then.

They say that things happen in a perfect way and in a second stage of contact with the Enneagram, I began seeing it as a map or starting point. Then I began a path that led to happiness and thanks to this tool, I've found endless guides during the journey and the most important learning: that there is no such thing as right or wrong. There are as many views as people on the planet. I've learned to respect other points of view, and that has given me the opportunity to meet and appreciate different kinds of people that I used to judge severely before. It was thanks to the Enneagram that I understood that my truth is not absolute and that it's only a partial vision of THE truth.

Since then, acceptance has been my best companion on this path of improvement. I accept that life is very diverse and not only what I learned as a child. I realized that people succeed in life not only by being good and hardworking, but above all by being happy, and seeking wellness for others.

It's hard to say, but I've learned to accept that being happy is good."

EDUARD *(Enneatype One)*

It was not until he changed his belief of "having to be good and right at all times" that this construct was relaxed and, although today he can perceive the drive to seek perfection, he no longer plays the role of judge and enjoys life fully.

This is the work proposed by the Enneagram, and that is why the changes are so dramatic, since they occur in the deepest layers of the procedural memory system and the attentional systems (ARAS).

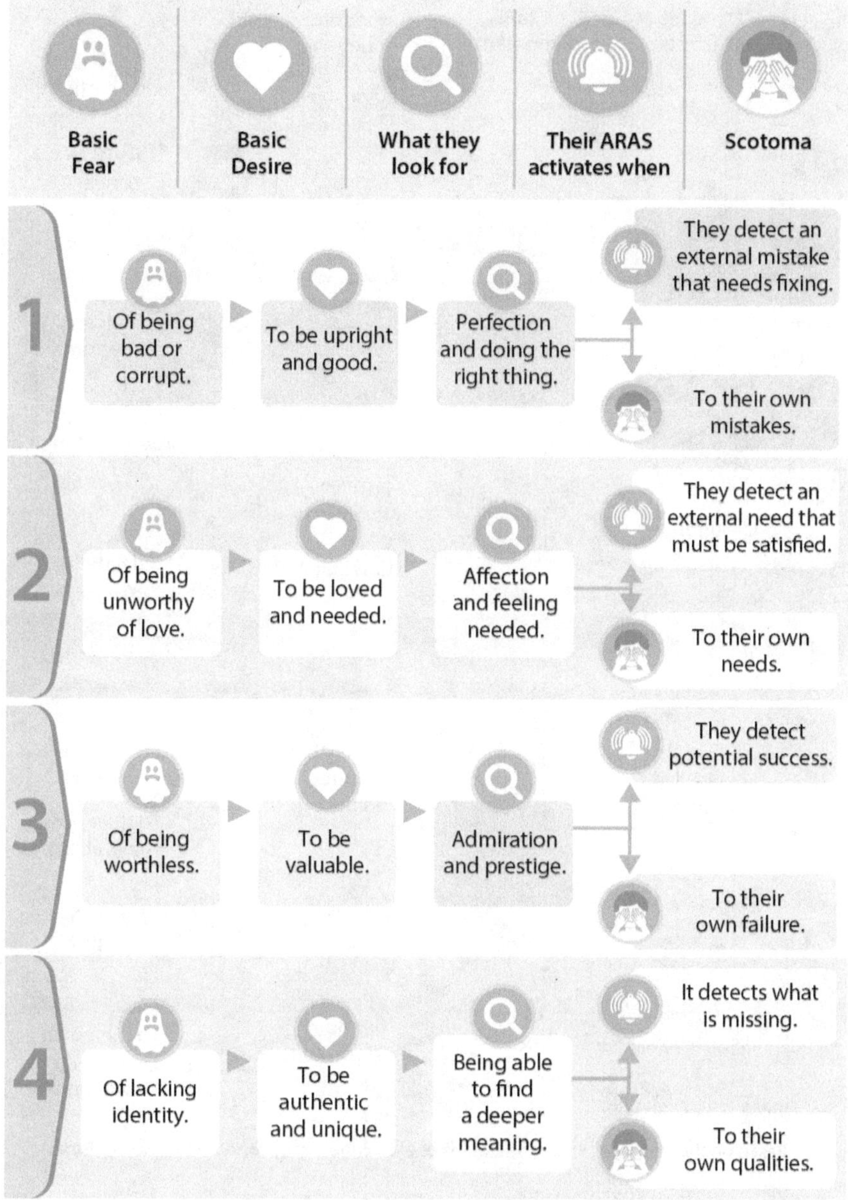

Based on the messages, fears and desires of each Enneatype proposed by Riso-Hudson.

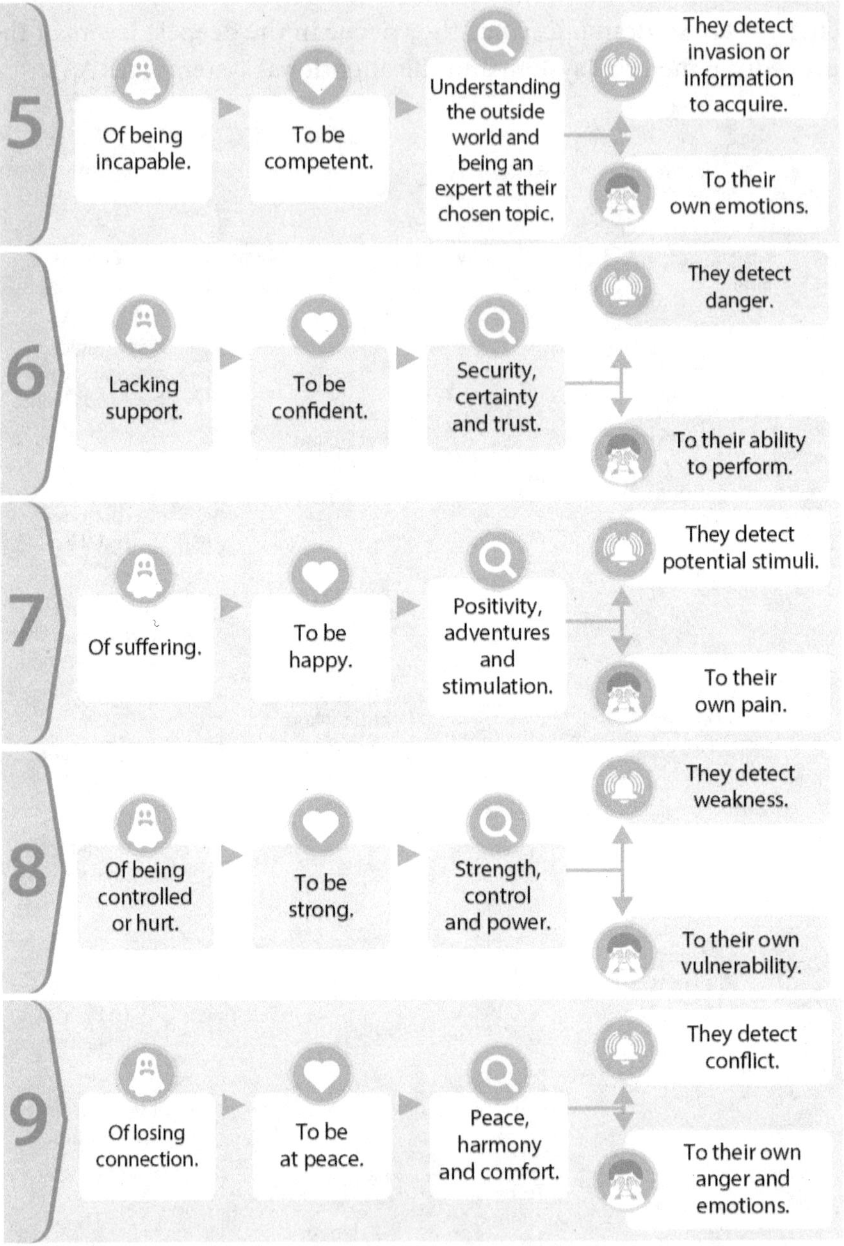

Based on the messages, fears and desires of each Enneatype proposed by Riso-Hudson.

How the ego builds reality

George Alexander Kelly, psychologist and educator, developed the philosophy of alternative constructivism. He put forth his theory of personal constructs in 1955. This theory maintains that, even though there is only one True Reality, it is always experienced from different perspectives.

These constructs are the representations of reality we make in order to use them as a reference pattern when making decisions. People construct an image of reality[24] based on their experience, which they assume is true, to understand their environment. From this perspective, they will develop strategies that ensure their survival.

QR video: How the brain creates reality?

https://youtu.be/ILDyGkYU-xQ

Kelly also suggests that people think following the scientific method. That is, they observe, experience and formulate a theory that when considered sufficiently proven, they accept as true without questioning it again. In order to act, the brain predicts situations using the information stored in the thalamus.

An example that can help us understand this theory is a baby discovering the force of gravity. The baby drops a toy, and it falls to the floor. We pick it up, give it to him, and he releases it again to see if it falls back to the ground. We can give it to him ten times in a row and the baby releases it again and again to see what happens. After observing enough times that when you drop the toy, it falls to the ground, the baby comes to the conclusion that every time you release the toy, it will fall to the ground. That is, he has formed a construct that will

---

[24] https://psiqueviva.com/cerebro-construye-nuestra-realidad/ (How the brain builds our reality).

serve as a reference for the rest of his life: *"When I drop something, it falls to the ground."*

The process that Kelly[25] suggests is the following: We observe a situation and then we proceed to search in our memory for a similar situation, because if the brain does not have a reference pattern, it does not know what to do with the information. Once we detect a reference, we act in a semi-automatic way according to the most successful action we previously had. This is also justified by the brain's biological need to reach maximum efficiency with minimal energy expenditure. That is why it does not waste large amounts of energy analyzing every situation separately, and instead looks for similar situations and acts according to them. If that strategy does not work, it creates a better one, discarding the old one.

According to this theory, we can assume that children observe their parents and start to develop strategies that allow them to guarantee care and protection as a result of being accepted and wanted by their caregivers.

That is, based on observation, they develop a personality that is desirable to their parents, adhering to those behaviors and attitudes throughout their lives. Since these are very old constructs, known as core constructs, they become the foundation of all our others, and will be the first reference point used to observe the world. When someone studies the Enneagram, they observe and question the constructs that they have automatically used throughout their life. If they realize that those constructs are not useful anymore, they actualize them, becoming aware that there are many more possibilities available to them.

Kelly maintained that reality is subject to various personal constructs, some useful and others not.

All of this is encompassed in one great process of constructing and reconstructing reality successively. It is related to what he called the Experience Cycle: an unending process whose results are directly linked to people's mental health. It consists of the following steps:

---

[25] Boaree, G. (2002). *Teorías de la personalidad (Personality Theories: From Freud to Frankl)*, Departamento de Psicología de la Universidad de Shippensburg, pp. 351.

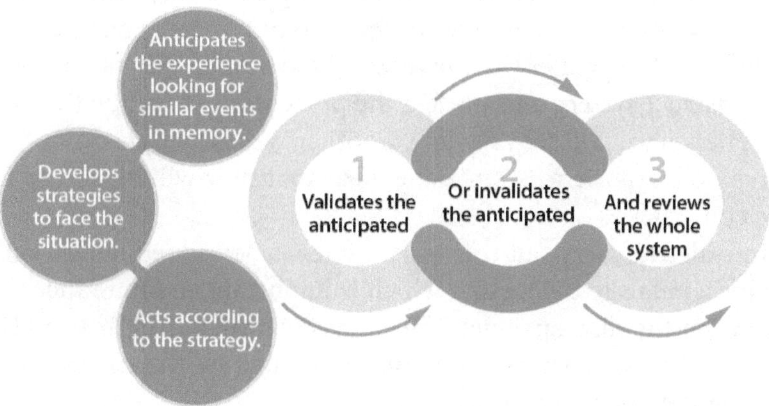

Kelly's experience cycle

According to the types of constructs Kelly mentions, it is possible to distinguish, from the Enneagram's perspective, the following construct types:

- **Core:** This manages the processes through which identity is maintained. It can be said that this construct contains our deepest beliefs. These beliefs provide meaning to the individual and, therefore, cannot be modified easily. This is precisely the type of construct to which the Enneatype belongs, and it can be modified when the person is aware of it. As long as we are not aware of this construct, it is nearly impossible to modify it.
- **Peripheral:** This stems from the previous construct type, although it enjoys greater flexibility, thus making it easy to modify.
- **Rigid:** This leads to invariable predictions, as can be the case of a generalization. It is typical of individuals with well-defined ideas, although it also appears in cases of obsession. This construct type can be related to the integration level of a person: the lower the integration of the personality, the greater the rigidity of the core construct.

Another concept that Kelly developed is the constriction of the construct system, a phenomenon that takes place when individuals reduce perception of themselves in order to minimize apparent incompatibilities. The greater their insecurity, the greater the constriction of the construct system and the less the perception of reality; that is, the awareness level will be very low. In other words, people do not want to live new experiences, since they fear that they will invalidate their core construct.

In order to carry out this task, a filter is developed which will allow individuals to detect that which is important and to reduce to the minimum the discrepancies with their construction of reality. These alert mechanisms are recorded and sustained by the ARAS, the Ascending Reticular Activating System.

How ego is upheld

The ego construct is formed during the first years of life, when children have little interaction with the world and their frame of reference is their close family nucleus. That is why the environment is quite stable, even if it is not nourishing or ideal. In other words: "*If my parents are violent, I will always expect a violent reaction, and my conclusion will be that the world is a violent place. For example, if I yell, my mom spanks me. Or, if I behave well, I am rewarded with a hug. I will conclude that love is conditional to certain behaviors. This is how I generate the basic belief that I will only be loved if I act in a certain way. I stop being me and begin to conform to what I believe my parents expect of me.*" Please notice I said: What I believe; constructs are not definitive because are based in a child's conclusion of the situation.

Once this response has been developed and tested, it passes to the subconscious and is stored in the procedural memory to be used throughout life whenever it is necessary. The subconscious always, in an effort to save energy and achieve greater chances of survival, develops a procedural manual that is stored in the procedural memory. Each time a similar situation occurs, the brain acts in the way it has previously worked automatically.

As an analogy: it's like riding a bicycle. Once you know how to do it, you do not re-analyze the movements involved; you just ride and act. In the same way, once you know what your parents expect from you, you only act automatically and, subsequently, do the same with other people. If it worked for you at age six, why would not it work with your boss now that you're 40?

Formation of somatic markers

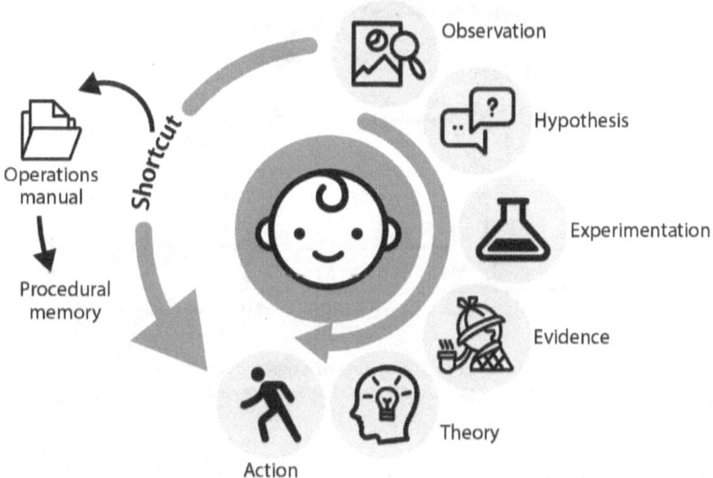

As we mentioned in the first chapter, our brain seeks to preserve our genes until the next generation, and as a result, will take it upon itself to reduce stress to a minimum to increase our chances of survival. So, based on the acceptance of our construct as being true, the brain adjusts reality by modifying perception, generating scotomas, or blind spots, to focus on the basic belief needed for survival, discarding anything it cannot handle or that does not agree with its mental frame of reference.

People see what they want to see, and their "reality" is a long way off from being THE REALITY, since it is a mere interpretation of what has happened to them throughout their life.

We can say that all inputs go through the attentional filter first, and that our attention is selective. Even though Broadbent's theory might not be shared by many, it seems to me an easy way of understanding what happens with the information that reaches our brain. The most conservative authors believe that our brain receives 400,000 bits of information a second, and that only 50 are processed consciously.

The brain must choose which information is to be analyzed to avoid going crazy. But how does it organize hierarchically what it pays attention to?

Broadbent's filter theory

EGO is an attentional system that decides which inputs are important in order to guarantee survival.

Because we have beliefs through which we select the inputs, there are many other inputs that are left out because our filter decides which information is relevant and which is not. The Enneagram helps us understand that the goal of that filter is to accomplish our biological survival.

The problem is that, according to what the Enneagram establishes, these filters are formed along with personality, which is developed during the first years of life. In other words, every one of us filters life selectively using a lens that we designed with the cognitive abilities of a child, when the neocortex is not fully developed.

More current is the proposal made by A. Damásio: a somatic marker is a set of behaviors that are repeated systematically and automatically when the same circumstances occur. These behaviors are the result of the child's experimentation in early childhood; that is, a survival process within the nuclear environment. The child learns that certain attitudes and behaviors are appreciated by his environment, and he executes them automatically to guarantee the care and affection he requires. We could say that personality is a kind of somatic marker. Next, we will take a look at how it works.

Emotions move us, beliefs hinder us

Emotions, as the name implies, are what set us in motion; and they can be defined from the neurobiological point of view as a set of stimuli, whether innate or acquired, that directly influence our bodily reactions, such as the heartbeat or the redness of the face. The drive of an instinct leads us to the physical expression of it. Damásio's classification places emotions in two categories:

1. **Primary:** (innate) are those that appear in babies and depend on the neural circuits that belong to the limbic system, where the amygdala and the cortex play a transcendent role. It is the basic mechanism of emotional behaviors (joy, anger, sadness, fear, disgust, etc.).
2. **Secondary:** (subtle or social) are the result of a relationship with the environment and involve mental interpretations of primary emotions. They seek our survival within the group and take us out of homeostasis or balance, so we must attend them as a priority.

Each personality manifests a certain set of secondary emotions that are known in the Enneagram as passions or blind spots.

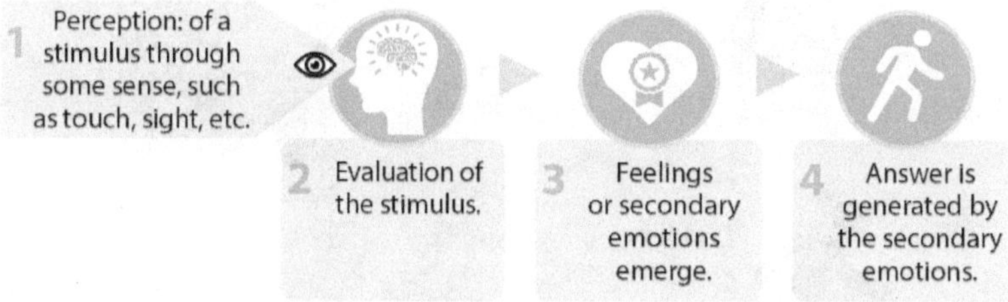

Emotions involve four steps:

1. **Perception**: of a stimulus through some sense, such as touch, sight, etc.
2. **Evaluation**: The stimulus or situation is evaluated and compared with similar previous situations by the limbic system.
3. **Secondary** emotions emerge and produce action in us.
4. **Answer**: we will find two types of response according to the risk involved:
   a. Rapid response: the reaction is directly activated without further analysis and is useful when there is an imminent danger such as fire or predators. This type of response is vital to survival and occurs within 100 milliseconds.
   b. Slow response: this type of response takes 300 milliseconds. In this case, the signal passes through the neocortex. The situation is evaluated more carefully to refine the response mechanisms. It is useful when there is no hurry to generate a reaction.

For example, we are walking down the street when we notice a long, dark shadow. For starters, we stop and take a step back, since we think it is a snake but, a few milliseconds later, we realize that it is actually a rope, so we continue our walk. The short response makes us react while the information is processed more thoroughly, and a long response is produced.

Response modes of the limbic system

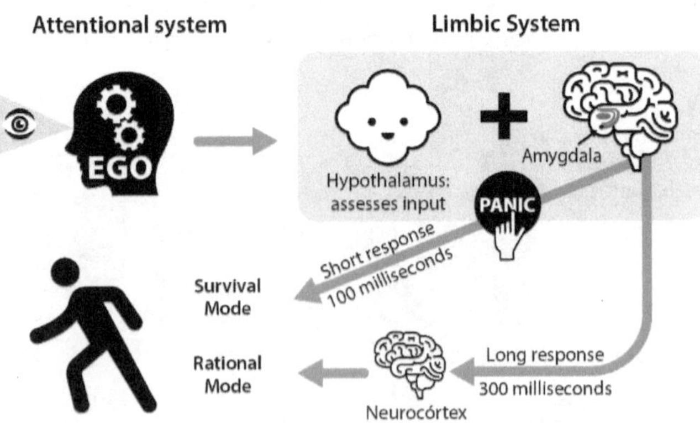

Somatic markers and the Enneagram

Emotions are linked to thinking to increase the effectiveness of survival responses. Damásio explains that somatic markers are a kind of thought guide or learned response.

They are the result of a relationship between the brain and culture. When we become aware of the nuclear perception of reality, the markers are deactivated. Our responses are no longer reactive, that is, generated by the amygdala, but are generated from reflection and analysis. These are much more appropriate, because they take into account the current environment and are not just automatic reactions to similar emotional situations.

When we receive punishments or rewards from our parents and others representing social conventions, we configure a range of responses to certain stimuli that are automatically marked in our system. This means that in the brain there are a series of somatic markers that are part of our reasoning and decision-making mechanisms. The cortex classifies the experiences lived and uses them to produce possible future scenarios that serve to guide our behavior and are related to the Enneatype.

These somatic markers are formed from an early age and orient our reactions to previously tested responses, discarding some alternatives and selecting others that are valued positively. Personality is precisely a somatic marker that governs our life unconsciously or without us knowing. It is a survival mechanism that developed in our early childhood and that, despite being dysfunctional, was efficient for the child.

The richness of the Enneagram consists of making these automatic response patterns conscious and allowing us to question them. As we saw earlier, the brain will automatically update these markers by contrasting them with reality. But if they do not become part of our awareness, they will continue to govern our lives, without our even knowing that they exist. That is why, once we know them, the changes in the level of relative well-being of people are so radical, since the brain updates them as a mechanism of adaptation and survival.

These markers were created by that helpless child who did not have tools such as language, physical strength or the ability to move to survive in an environment that he did not understand and could help him to relate to his protective figures. That is why, when we become aware of them, the brain updates them by adding the range of tools that we as the adult possess. In Enneagram terms, it is called the integration process, and it is nothing more than making the limbic system less reactive and making greater use of the slow response to situations that ceased to be potentially dangerous.

Reviewing the brain structures that are affected and involved in the formation of each personality construct will remain a subject for further research. But what we do know empirically is that, if the individual has a self-image of helplessness, he will wait and even demand that the environment meets his needs. For this, somatic personality markers were created; these are nothing more than reactions that resulted to ensure that the helpless child's needs were met by their caregivers.

The moment the nuclear construct of the Enneatype is modified, the individual takes control of his life, because he no longer has the limiting belief that was a reality in his childhood. When deactivating somatic markers, he begins to integrate tools such as assertive language, analysis and reflection. This provides a greater sense of autonomy and reduced reactivity. Somatic markers will activate less as the perception of helplessness decreases. Although I've noticed, and neuroscience confirms, that in the moment a person perceives themselves as helpless again, the markers that had fallen into disuse will reactivate. Yet, being aware of them and knowing that we have other tools, the reaction is shorter and less intense.

The greater the stress, the greater the focus of attention, the greater the reactivity and the lower the capacity to respond. Daniel Goleman[26] states that the human brain uses the same mechanisms to confront psychological pain that have been used for thousands of years to deal with dangerous situations and that it is closely related to the approach of Carl Jung, Swiss psychiatrist and psychologist, about the collective unconscious representing a series of responses that humans have used throughout the history of mankind in certain situations and that have

---

[26] Goleman, D. (2016), *El punto ciego (Vital lies, simple truth)*. Me gusta leer, p. 55.

been inherited unconsciously, without being taught directly. In this way, Goleman concludes that the key element of the response to stress is not so much the danger, **but the perception of defense against such danger.**

A research team from the University of California at Los Angeles carried out a study that consisted of applying electric shocks to rats; the first group could not avoid such shocks in any way, while the second group could avoid them. What they discovered in the end was that the shocks were less threatening to the rats that knew that they could do something to avoid them.

Personality can be seen as a cognitive process that develops in early childhood, through which all the information we receive throughout life is processed and which responds to the child's need to rely on adults to provide for their needs.

Radical changes in the perception of reality that people have before and after knowing the Enneagram have been observed by making this cognitive behavioral pattern conscious. The individual ceases to respond automatically to the environment, begins a process of analysis without bias and responds in a better way through new learning processes. To do this, we must understand that the perceptual patterns of each personality are designed for the survival of the individual, by being accepted by their protective figures.

These patterns of perception are registered in the limbic system and selectively search for relevant information for this purpose, leaving without analyzing what is not considered significant by the attention system. When the information or input is perceived as risky for survival, the amygdala triggers the "survival" mechanism and disconnects the neocortex, giving a quick response to the input received.

The Enneagram helps us understand the nine different attentional filters that define the information that is relevant to survival and through which life is perceived. From my point of view, it is not so much the learning style but the systems of attention and motivation which are different, and these are perfectly described in the Enneagram. Knowing the Enneagram, in my opinion, increases emotional intelligence and improves human relationships of all kinds.

CHAPTER 5

What is integration?

Dan Siegel's theory of the integrated brain and the Enneagram

Dan Siegel is a doctor and a clinical professor of psychiatry at the UCLA School of Medicine. He is also a pioneer in the field of interpersonal neurobiology, and wrote the book *The Whole-Brain Child*. He talks about neural or brain integration. Dr. Siegel explains in a very straight-forward way what neural or brain integration (a much-used, well-known term in the Enneagram that refers to the level of reactivity or consciousness of a person) consists of, using a hand to explain his model of the brain.[27]

QR video: Dr Dan Siegel presenting a hand model of the brain

https://www.youtube.com/watch?v=gm9CIJ74Oxw

Siegel explains that if we look at a hand with its palm towards us, the palm and the forearm would represent the spine. As the thumb closes upon the palm, it would become the equivalent of the limbic brain, and its fingernail would represent the brain amygdala. This amygdala is responsible for the detection and triggering of dangerous situations, which require a fast response, as we mentioned in the previous chapter. Its objective is to trigger the alarm mechanism to act

---

[27] If you wish to know more about this theory, you can watch Dan Siegel's talk on his hand model here: https://www.youtube.com/watch?v=LiyaSr5aeho

fast when there is no time for the neocortex to run a thorough test of the situation. This is called a "disintegrated brain".

If we close our hand over our thumb, and look at it sideways, we will have a model much alike the brain, where the remaining four fingers represent the rational part of the brain, known as the neocortex. When the hand is closed, it represents the brain in rational mode, which means that the neocortex is in charge of processing information and acting in an integrated manner.

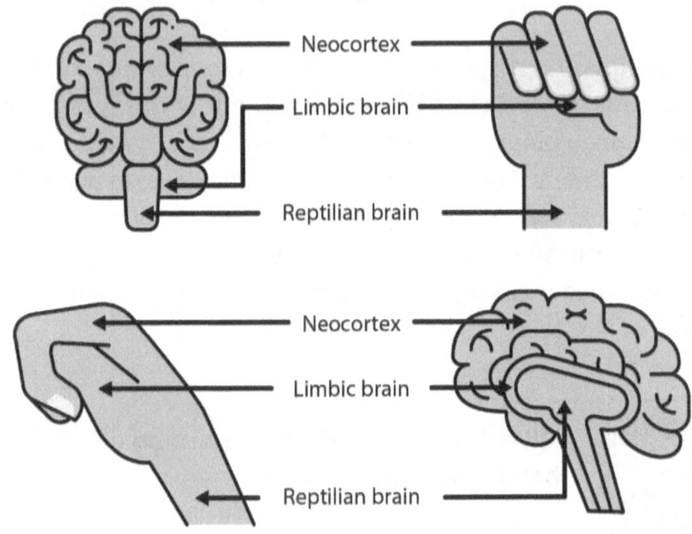

According to this model, when we are in survival or **reactive mode**, meaning in the hands of the limbic brain and the brain amygdala, our neocortex disconnects, and we operate only with the primitive part of the brain: the reptilian brain.

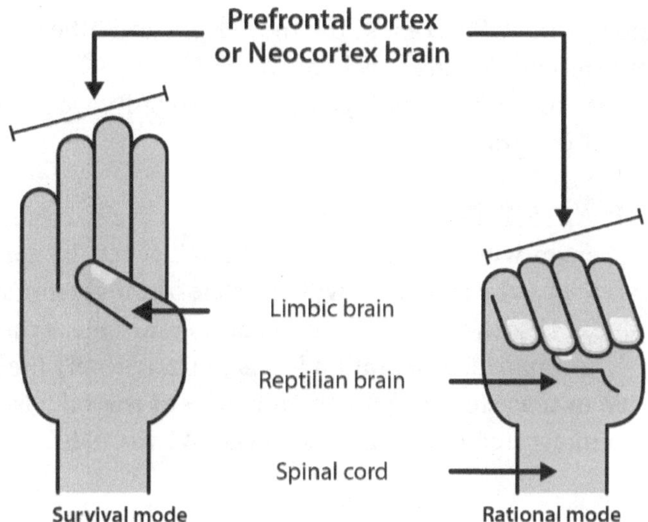

Regarding these two operation modes, it seems only natural to recall Gurdjieff, who said that in order to contact our essence, we should have all three integrated centers. In other words, that our head, heart and gut centers are coordinated and integrated. This is equivalent to the integrated brain that Siegel talks about; an integrated brain is what allows us to contact our essence.

Integration levels[28]

Consciousness can be defined as the ability of being aware of what happens inside us and around us. Therefore, the level of consciousness or integration will be determined by the degree of interconnection between the different brain areas of the individual and by the adequate synaptic connection of the senses so he can perceive external and internal stimuli in a non-scotomic manner. This will provide greater ability to perceive reality without distortion. Or, looking at it from the opposite direction, the more threatened the person feels, the

---

[28] The elaboration of the features that make up each type was originally done by Don Riso in 1977 and later developed together with Russ Hudson in the 1990s.

more scotomas he will have and the more rigid and inflexible his behavior patterns and defense mechanisms will be.

To facilitate the understanding of each personality, we will describe three levels of integration:

- **HEALTHY** personality or integrated levels: correspond to a person with a lot of emotional intelligence. In the spiritual area, it can be compared with the state of enlightenment or holiness. Less than 2% of the population is usually at these levels.

  Comparing integration levels to Dan Siegel's theory, people in these levels make the majority of their decisions with an integrated brain or in "**RATIONAL MODE**".

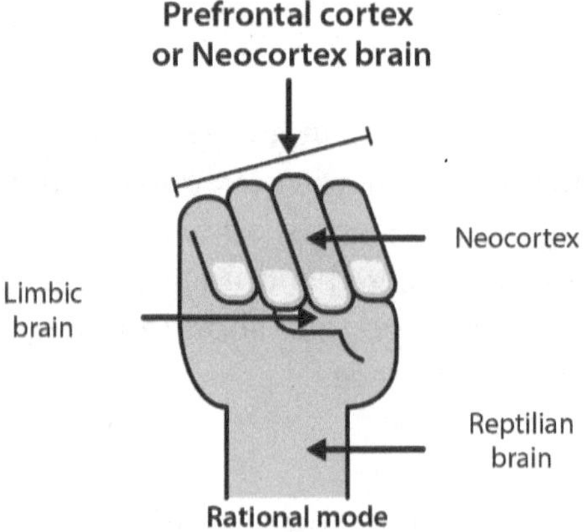

- **Average level:** refers to the typical characteristics of each Enneatype, where the person lives without questioning himself too much, doing what he has always done and obtaining the usual results. The personality or ego is in "**AUTOMATIC MODE**". Most people are here.
- **TOXIC personality** or disintegrated levels: These levels describe the instinctive reactions or disintegrated behaviors of each Enneatype. These are people with a very low level of consciousness, that mainly react rather than respond. According to Dan Siegel's model, they are people in "**SURVIVAL MODE**".

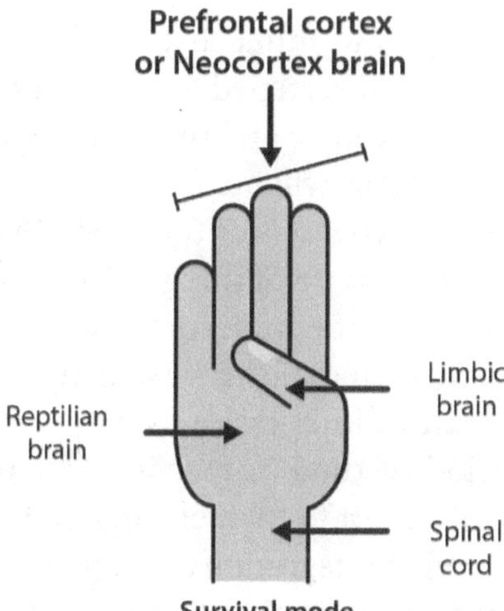

Behind each Enneatype there is an internal structure that sustains the personality and for which the Enneagram describes the predictable behaviors, attitudes and defenses. The levels explain the differences between people of the same Enneatype, as well as the different ways they behave in the face of different levels of threat.

This tool can help therapists and counselors identify what their patients are experiencing to guide them to find better options for their lives, as well as help leaders to manage and develop the talent of their teams within organizations.

What is your level of integration?

The Enneagram describes nine basic survival strategies of the human being that predetermine their selective attention systems, scotomas and mechanisms for sustaining attention towards what guarantees it. As we have already seen, each personality or Enneatype is based on a belief that generates a basic fear of death and, therefore, a basic desire to compensate for that fear. As I mentioned earlier, the level of integration of an individual will depend on the level of stress or helplessness he perceives. That is, the personality will manifest itself more as the threat perception increases.

That is why it is logical to think that, if all reality is based on the need to survive, the more threatened the person feels, the more rigid their defense mechanism will be and the more predictable and inflexible their behavioral patterns will be.

I want to distinguish two states of the level of integration:

What I call the **chronic state of integration,** is the level that a person exhibits most of the time under normal conditions and which generally presents a characteristic brain structure.

The **temporary state of integration** is the level that a person presents for a short period of time in reaction to temporary situations. After a while, they will revert to their chronic state of integration. The higher the chronic level of integration or awareness, the faster the person will return to it after having undergone a process of temporary disintegration.

For example, someone who presents low levels of integration can be strongly affected and remain disintegrated for long periods after an event that would be inconsequential for other people. Let's say you have a traffic altercation and do not recover your balance in a week, and not before telling a dozen people about the event to and feeling like a victim because of it. On the other hand, a person with a high chronic level of integration before the same altercation might temporarily disintegrate but recovers his chronic state in a short time and leaves the event behind them and gets on with their life.

The Enneagram states that human beings have both essence and personality or ego. In my opinion, the Enneagram describes the way each personality is formed to defend the essence of Being and helps us lead with a threatening environment. It also explains why, as the environment becomes more threatening, the ego structure becomes more rigid. Thus, we see that when we descend to lower levels of integration, the potential of the human being will be increasingly limited.

In summary and according to Kelly, each of us builds a model of reality that we use as a frame of reference to anticipate situations and achieve the greatest chances of survival. This model corresponds to our Enneatype. When we introduce self-observation, by raising awareness of the existence of the personality construct, we begin to question it, and adapt it to our current situation.

While disintegration occurs unconsciously, working with the Enneagram involves recovering brain integration through conscious work with the characteristic fears of each level.

The Enneagram is a dynamic tool that describes the changing nature of personality patterns. Although many Enneagram teachers have concerns about the levels of integration that Riso Hudson describe, I think that they are helpful to explain the relation between the pathology of each personality and the high levels of consciousness. It allows us to understand the process of human development as a constant path of evolution or involution that, in turn, serves as a guide for human development processes.

Knowing the levels of each Type, seeing how they are interrelated and that healthy traits can deteriorate in people that are not so healthy, can help us understand how the ego takes control over our life little by little.

Personal Integration Thermometer

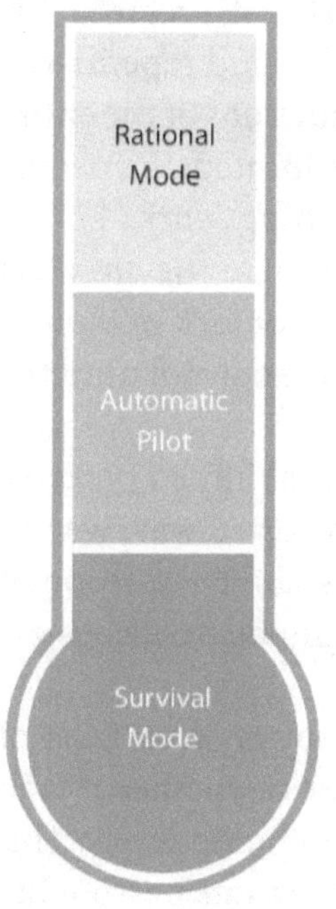

- Everything flows in your life and you always seek excellence.
- You are independent, and do not expect the solutions from others.
- You contribute new ideas and support others.
- You are clear that everyone's well-beings in your own well-being.
- You are very committed to your surroundings.
- You are extremely proactive.
- You know that your happiness is your responsibility.

- You fulfill your obligations, with no problem.
- Many times you live on autopilot.
- You think "others" cause you problems.
- You manipulate people to give you what you want, or defend from being manipulate by others.
- You live stressed and surrounded by conflicts.
- You believe that others have to make you happy.

- You demand that others meet your needs.
- Everyone is against you.
- You are openly aggressive and people are not comfortable with you.
- You spend 30% of your productive energy on complaints and "gossip."
- You have a hard time feeling respect from others.
- You live watching your back so that nobody abuses you.
- Your motto is: "I have to survive, at whatever price."
- Other have an obligation to make you happy.

The Enneagram is a dynamic system and is far from being a mere categorization of people, so linking it to the stress level will help us understand how we can modify our behaviors by changing our perception of reality. I like to compare the personality with a building, we can go up and down, depending on the level of threat we perceive in the different situations that are presented to us throughout the day. The floors of the building correspond to the different levels of integration.

When we are in the upper floors of the building in the executive suite, from which we have a great perspective and the horizon is wider, we have the ability to perceive reality in a way that is less distorted by our attention systems. While there, we make better decisions and respond appropriately to the challenges that life presents us. I call this state the **rational mode**.

The average level would be comparable to the intermediate floors of the building, where the company's operations department is located, all the processes are very defined and resources are optimized to achieve results in the shortest time and at the lowest cost. I refer to this state as **automatic mode**, since processes are routine and repetitive.

In the basement of the building we find the foundations of the entire building. This is where maintenance managers are located, the people who provide the services that ensure that everything works so the organization can continue operating. We call this state the **survival mode** since, during an emergency (such as flooding or lack of electrical energy), its function, like that of the ego, is to take control until the situation returns to normal again.

If we remember that the levels are related to the ability to perceive the stimuli of the environment in a more or less distorted way; we can say that the rational mode describes the person's ability to respond adequately to a given situation, while the survival mode describes the automatic reaction patterns of the Enneatype.

To understand a person, it is necessary to know at what level of integration they are at a given time. One must assess whether it is in its integrated, average or disintegrated range of operating levels. This is important because, for example, two people of the same personality type differ significantly if one is healthy and the other toxic. And also, the same person can move along the levels during the day depending on the situation they are in. If they perceive a threat, they will react in "survival mode" or from the reptilian response, while, if they are in a friendly environment, they will behave according to what is described as the healthy or integrated level of their personality, that which we know as the "rational mode." For both relationships and education, understanding this distinction is vital.

The Enneatype generates a brain structure that allows the individual to adapt in a certain reality. Through the processes of synaptic pruning and synaptic hyperconnectivity, it will generate scotomas towards any situation that belies the nuclear construction and will develop selective attention to what, in its opinion, provides a greater chance of survival.

As a result of this, they will develop a characteristic brain structure[29] that will be based on the stimulation and exchanges of the child with the outside world during the first years of life. Integration implies the creation of new neuronal circuits that will also cause the appearance of new functions that, in turn, will allow us to interact more adequately with the environment.

Culture modifies cognitive processes but, above all, the perception and prioritization of objects, events and phenomena. It is an instrument of adaptation to the environment in which one lives. Human beings transform what surrounds us, but we are also transformed by what we build to adapt. The brain, therefore, is modified by our own cultural interaction with the environment[30].

Another thing to consider that alters the perception of reality, is that when the brain evokes a memory, it becomes unstable, similar to a computer file. When it is saved again, the updated version of the previous memory is saved. We add new sensations to the old memory every time we remember, that is why the more a story is told, the more it is misrepresented until it differs completely from the original. This same characteristic is what we use in the Enneagram to update

---

[29] Portellano, J. (2008), *Introducción a la Neuropsicologia (Introduction to Neuropsychology)*, McGraw-Hill, p.37.

[30] Frade, L. (2011), *Diseño de situaciones didácticas (Design of teaching situation)*, Calidad Educativa, p. 38.

the answers and modify the basic belief of survival. Through the development of the internal observer towards the Enneatype reactions, people realize that painful or dangerous memories are no longer such and can then modify the somatic markers of their personality.

For example, the Nine's ARAS system will be activated by any conflict signal that is detected, either to solve it, or to leave that signal out of the person's attentional system, and thus avoiding its involvement in an unsolvable conflictive situation. In other words, an attentional filter generates a scotoma or blind spot regarding conflict situations. That is why Nines consider themselves as distracted, but in reality, they learned from a very young age to let go of conflicting feelings to be at peace.

Among the stimuli that Nines learn to let go are their own basic needs. In other words, they lose contact with their body, by disconnecting themselves from their bodily sensations and seem to be numb to life. This situation is very painful for the Nines and, therefore, they also disconnect from their emotions to survive.

I would dare to go even further, stating that the brain prunes painful stimuli as well. Here's what Carlos Belmonte[31] says regarding pain:

> *Besides, from the higher areas of the central nervous system projections are sent, which act on the neurons of the spinal cord that receive information from nociceptors, being able to inhibit it, thus preventing pain messages from reaching the brain cortex. This ability of the nervous system to cut the passing of painful information in an ascending direction is the basis of diverse phenomena, such as the absence of pain during life-threatening situations (fighting, fleeing), and, in part, during hypnosis or acupuncture.* (p. 2)

In our example of Nines, since their needs will not be noticed, they do not want to, or cannot, see them. My theory is that synaptic pruning of the painful experience is performed, even if sensations are perceived,

---

[31] Belmonte, C. (2014), El dolor, ¿mecanismo de defensa o castigo? (Pain, Punishment or defense mechanism?), conferencia.

as Belmonte mentions when referring to the syndrome of indifference to pain:

> *"That occurs due to a lesion in a cortical region. The channels that give pain its affective and unpleasant touch are not the same than those in charge of informing that a lesion has been inflicted. One or the other can be altered, and, if the affective mechanisms do not activate, the person does no perceive the stimulus as particularly unpleasant.[32]"*

Nines use being indifferent to their bodily sensations and pain as a survival mechanism, and the last thing they need is for other people to remind them how disconnected they are, since they will only feel greater disconnection, suffering and estrangement. Based on the above statements, it is logical to think that the brain structure of each personality would have to present certain structural characteristics. In other words, according to the Enneatype, an increase in connections in certain areas and disconnections in others can be predicted.

To Nines, life itself depends on others taking care of them and providing them with what they need. They live with the feeling of being incapable of providing sustenance for themselves and often worry more about providing for others so later others will provide back. Of course, this automatic mechanism to do for others, so that they will later do for me, is absurd from the outside. But considering that this mental model was formed during childhood, we will be able to understand this is the reality frame for Nines.

In the groups I work with, I have witnessed impressive and profound changes in people once they consciously question the usefulness of their core construct, and afterwards update it according to their current situation.

In summary, according to Kelly, human beings build a model of reality that, to us, corresponds to the Enneatype, and we later on use it

---

[32] https://www.lainformacion.com/tecnologia/carlos-belmonte-el-dolor-tambien-esuna-reconstruccion-del-cerebro 6G6J2WS5k3Ph0J1Yz4LYP4/

as a frame of reference to anticipate situations and achieve the greatest possibilities of survival. When we introduce the observation effect, we gain awareness of the existence of the core construct of personality. It will then be put to the test and questioned. People will see whether the construct is functional in their current life, and, when they discover that it brings more trouble than benefits, they naturally make the necessary changes.

Let us go back to the example of Nines: as children they realized that their needs would not be seen nor met, so they developed a mechanism to increase their chances of survival: minimizing their needs and waiting for others to provide the sustenance they required. In other words, they learned to keep quiet and to please others to guarantee their own survival.

The construct was made around the following beliefs:

- My needs are not important. Therefore, I am not important.
- It is not useful to get angry or to set boundaries.
- I depend on others liking me so they can satisfy my needs.

Cognitive-behavioral patterns typical of the Nine personality will not be deactivated until the brain has a new perspective that allows it to discard these constructs and to replace them with more efficient ones. This is done by modifying the "my needs are NOT important" basic belief, and transforming them into others that say *"my needs ARE important", and "I am important"*.

Riso-Hudson's levels of development

Most Enneagram teachers in the world recognize that there are different levels of integration or behavior in the same Enneatype, but it is Don Riso and Russ Hudson who first proposed the theory that there are nine levels of personality integration. Although many Enneagram teachers do not agree with them because they think that this theory does not have a scientific basis and that the number of levels was made arbitrarily, I think the approach is very helpful to understand the personality as a progressive mechanism that restricts our perception of reality gradually and continuously as our perception of helplessness or vulnerability increases. This theory gives the Enneagram a dynamism that makes it versatile and adaptable. Like all theories, the levels are not exact, but I include them because they help us understand the way in which the ego seizes the essence of a person little by little in its eagerness to protect itself

Recall that, like elevators, we can constantly go up and down through this continuum of personality. We will begin its description by the integrated levels, explaining the way in which the ego is generated, although we must take into account that children, although they are not disintegrated, do not have the high level of consciousness that we mentioned, since for that they would require a developed neocortex.

Integrated levels

LEVEL 1. Liberation

This level is not reached automatically but only with personal work. The individual has already left their self-image, worked with their basic fear and overcome it, so they are at a point of liberation and transcendence of the ego and begin to know its true essence. At this point they meet their real needs in the right way. The ego has become transparent and flexible and allows their spiritual virtues and abilities to emerge. These processes lead to balance, wisdom, strength and courage.

Traits of each Enneatype in this level

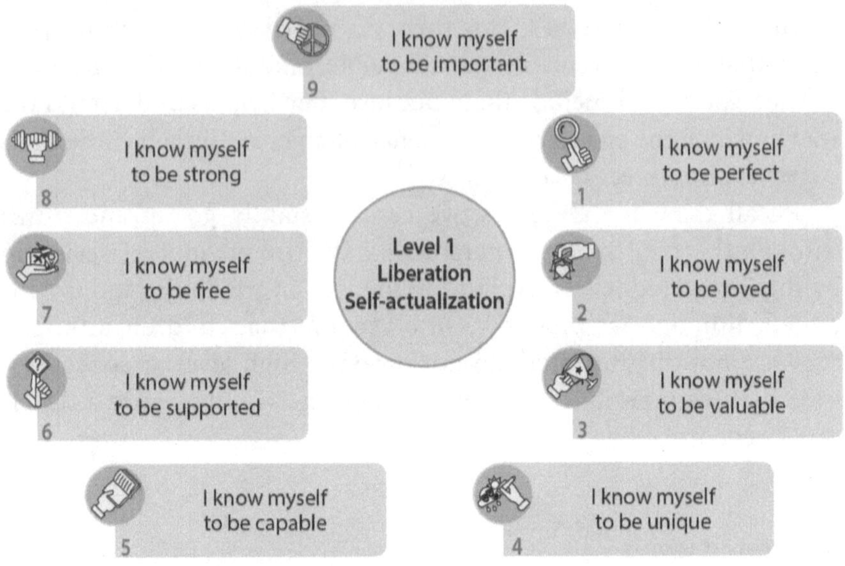

Based on *Understanding the Enneagram*, Riso-Hudson (2000).

LEVEL 2. Psychological capacity

At this level the individual is quite close to congruence, since they have a great capacity for self-observation. They are not free from the ego, but can detect it and realize how and when it is activated. The basic desire appears as a reaction to compensate for the basic fear of the Type, instead of returning to essence and relaxing the defense mechanism. This is how the nuclear construct of the ego or the ideal self is formed, with the believe that "when I reach or get X, it will be fine."

The idealized image of each Enneatype

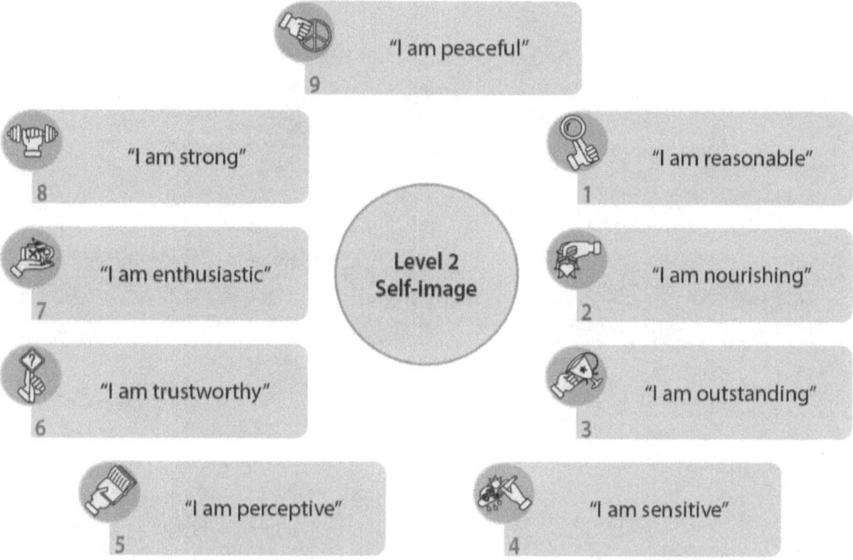

Based on *Understanding the Enneagram*, Riso-Hudson (2000).

LEVEL 3. Social value

This is still a very healthy level. At this level, people are enthusiastic and have great concern for society and for others. People and their essence are already protected by the ego's defense mechanisms, but we can still see the good traits of the Enneatype at a social level. In other words, we can observe a certain level of disintegration as a person but they still are highly functional in the social and work spheres. These people are very concerned with making a better world.

My contribution to the world

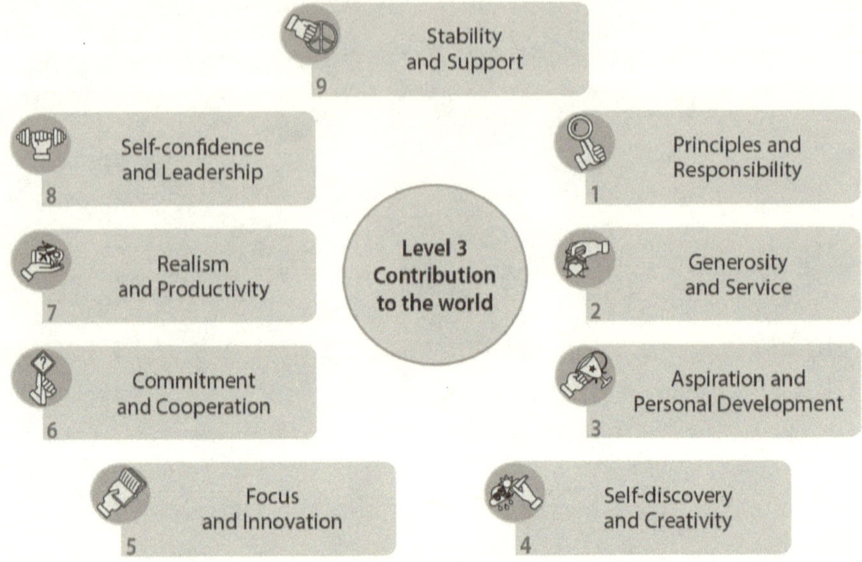

Based on *Understanding the Enneagram*, Riso-Hudson (2000).

Average levels

Past this point we have what Riso-Hudson call the *wake-up call*: An ensemble of certain behaviors that begin to appear repeatedly, serving as a warning to know that the ego is becoming active and that we are moving away from our essence.

The wake-up call of each Enneatype

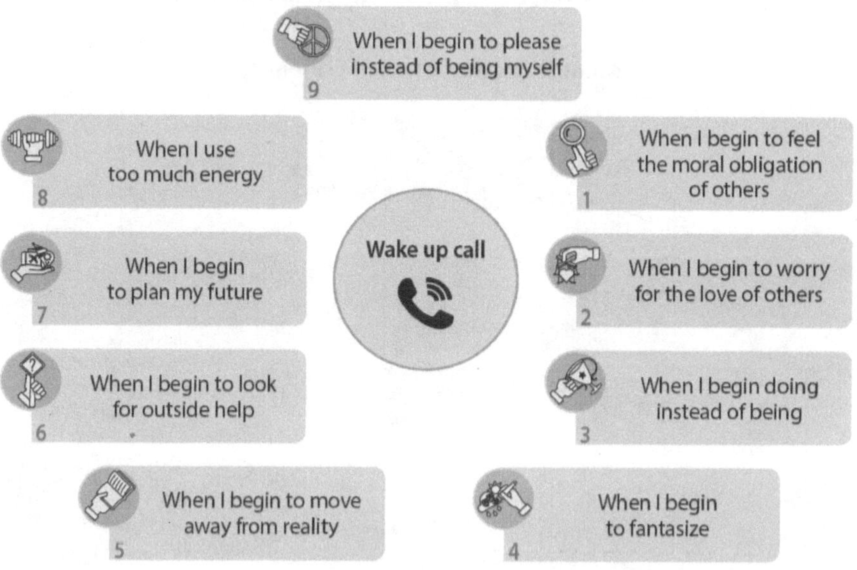

Based on *Understanding the Enneagram*, Riso-Hudson (2000).

LEVEL 4. Imbalance

At this level, people are still pleasant, but they are getting swallowed up by the "social role". They give up on themselves and lose conscious awareness of their real potential. They do what is expected of them and they take many things for granted. Their life depends on being someone's wife, someone's father, someone's boss...The belief is: *"If my social role is ok, then I am ok"*. And the mental fixation typical to each Enneatype appears. They begin to develop selective attention to satisfy that fixation. Even though they still have some flexibility and freedom not to be trapped in the structures of the ego, they have few resources at their disposal, and passion begins to show.

People on this level are concerned with their social position, the place they have in the company; they want to be everyone's favorite. They no longer know unconditionality.

Once this point is reached, their self-observation ability is reduced and clear changes are noticeable towards identification with the ego.

Their cognitive pattern will be distorted by fixation and despite ego not causing problems yet, it is on the way to cause them.

Mental fixation of each Enneatype

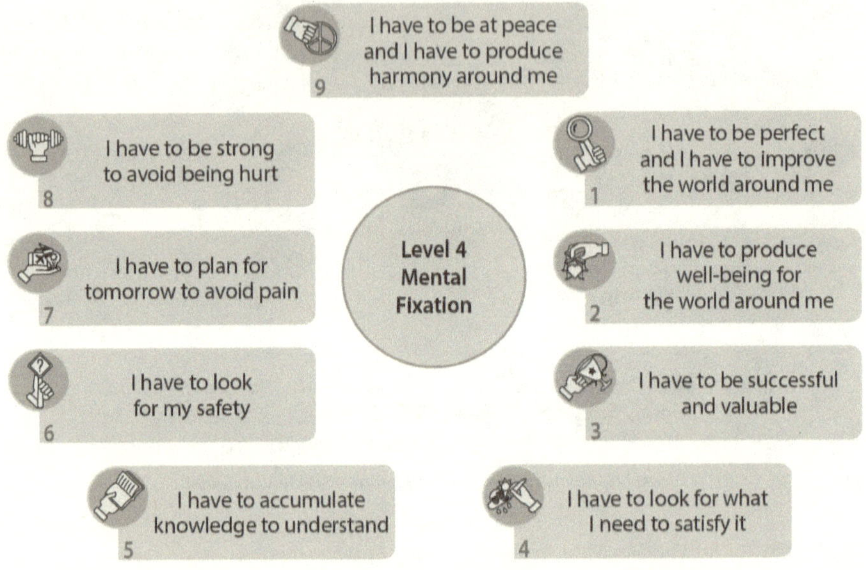

Based on *Understanding the Enneagram*, Riso-Hudson (2000).

LEVEL 5. Interpersonal control

At this point, people begin to manipulate their environment so it adjusts to the demands of their ego; they use others to satisfy their needs. They want others to think and feel in a certain way to fulfill their expectations. In these levels there are many hidden messages and a lot of negativity. The name of the game is power. Nothing is said openly, but people constantly manipulate each other to satisfy their basic need, or they spend their time defending themselves to avoid being manipulated.

Manipulation strategies of each Enneatype

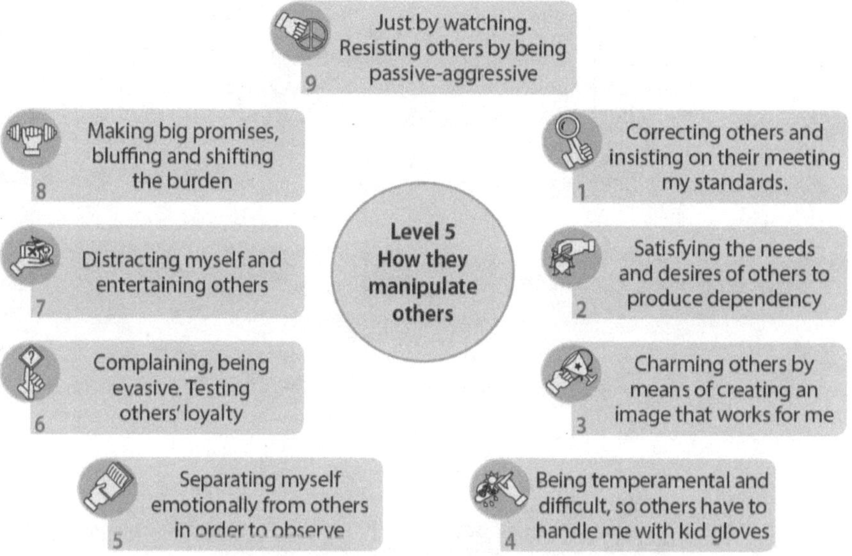

Based on *Understanding the Enneagram*, Riso-Hudson (2000).

LEVEL 6. Overcompensation

At this level, people feel at a disadvantage and justified in demanding that their environment meet their needs. They do not care whether it is good or bad, they want it anyway. They do to others what they would be afraid of being done to them.

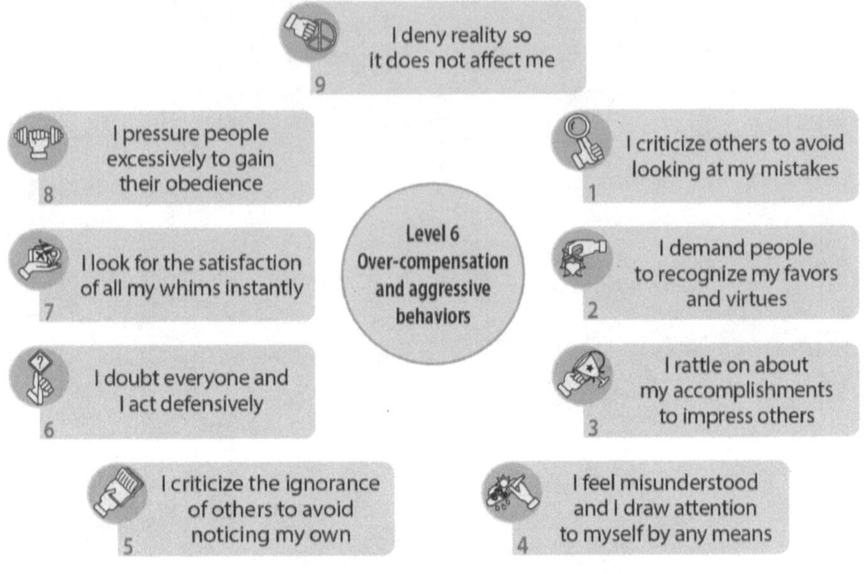

Based on *Understanding the Enneagram*, Riso-Hudson (2000).

Disintegrated levels

Passing from average to disintegrated levels results in disintegration of the third intelligence center. Reaching this point implies the loss of the ability to perceive reality without distortion through any given center, since in disintegrated levels all three centers have a distorted perception of reality. Some kind of therapeutic or spiritual support is needed to be able to regain integration. For example, the program of Alcoholics Anonymous works because people who are at these levels have the accompaniment of someone who gives them this point of reference of reality and allows them to observe their situation from a less distorted angle. From this point onwards, people begin to walk away due to the difficulty of being around someone at these levels, pathologies and personality disorders begin to manifest.

All the Enneatypes have gifts that can become self-destructive for them and others at these levels. Negative behaviors are a desperate attempt to keep their sense of identity, and defend themselves from a hostile world created by the Enneatype's constructs, which in these levels are particularly rigid. They experience a series of out-of-control reactions and illusions. People do not find a solution to the fear, problems and conflicts they have brought upon themselves, which is why they react more intensively and put even more pressure on the environment, looking for the satisfaction of their needs.

LEVEL 7. Violation

At this level, people seek to maintain their personality structures at all costs, and are willing to do anything in order to accomplish it. Addictions to substances, people or situations begin here. People on this level are desperate; they have lost the ability to respond by themselves, and they need help. The perception of helplessness is such that they feel justified to act in very nonfunctional ways. People at this level cannot take responsibility for their behavior due to the scotomas that their ego has generated. In their effort to defend their egoic constructs, they become increasingly fragile, and sacrifice both their own and others' fundamental values.

Addictions at this Level

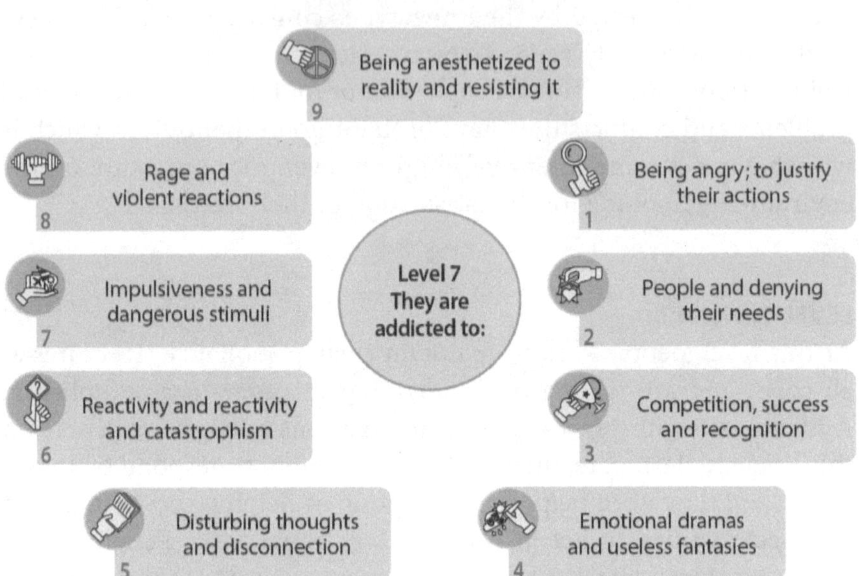

Based on *Understanding the Enneagram*, Riso-Hudson (2000).

LEVEL 8. Dilution and compulsion

Profound pathologies are developed in order to protect the feeble ego from threats. There is massive denial and repression. Identification with the ego is so deep, that reality must be rejected and denied; they fight against it. People on this level are not able to hear, listen or perceive reality, so arguing with them is useless.

Dilutions of each Enneatype

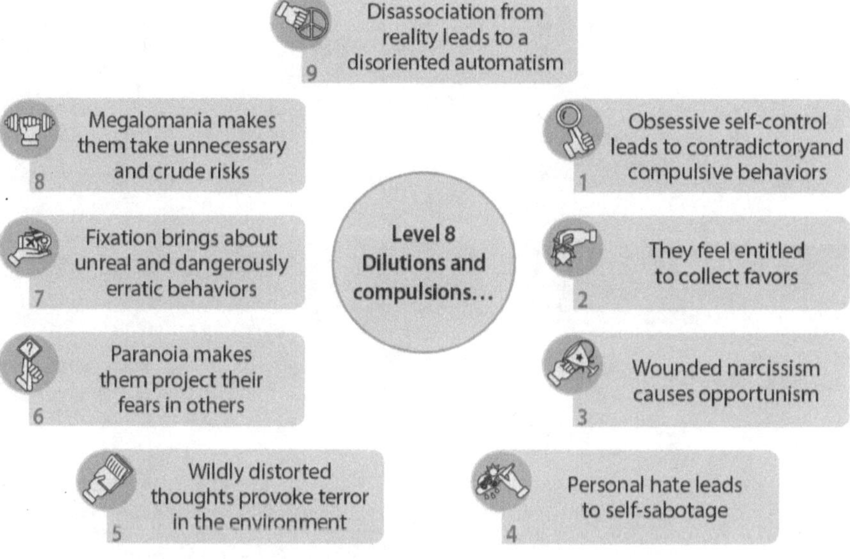

Based on *Understanding the Enneagram,* Riso-Hudson (2000).

LEVEL 9. Pathological destruction

On this level ego collapses. The ego's emptiness and uselessness lead people to seek for complicity in others or self-destruction.

The basic fear comes true

Based on *Understanding the Enneagram*, Riso-Hudson (2000).

Here is a case of how the process of disintegration looks like in daily life. A student shared an unpleasant legal experience with someone we will call Clara, a woman with Enneatype Six.

Clara's daughter improperly registered some stories that were commissioned to her as if she was the owner of the original idea. It was an easy administrative issue to solve, her daughter only had to appear and clarify the mistake. But since she had an unpleasant experience with the authority a little before, Clara focused on preventing her daughter from having to face the authorities at all costs. This caused the problem to grow disproportionately, since she was not able to hear anyone telling her that her daughter was not in danger. She could not trust even her closest friends, and in order to protect her, she disintegrated to the extent that she declared in front of a judge with the certainty that she was telling the truth that it was her idea to ask her daughter for the stories.

Her brain generated so many scotomas to maintain "her truth" that she was not able to hear all the reasoning and evidence that people close to her did. In fact, she constantly commented that she was incapable of lying with the absolute tranquility. Maybe this was true before this event, but when someone feels threatened, they need to defend their truth at whatever cost and cannot do anything differently.

The only way to achieve dialogue with someone at these levels is to reduce the level of stress so that they can return to the necessary brain integration that allows them to reason again; that is, to deactivate **survival mode** so they can return to **rational mode**.

Understanding the levels makes it clear that the way we act is based on the level of threat we perceive from the environment and that they are not processes independent of the environment, but the result of a need for adaptation and survival. Understanding the fears generated by these behaviors or reactions allows us to change the paradigms from where we move.

Another important consideration is that the chronic level of integration that adults present is directly related to the levels of threat or violence that they experienced during childhood, that is, the more the child perceived helplessness, the more their disintegration as an adult will be.

How are integration levels and Maslow's hierarchy of needs integrated?

Abraham Maslow, an American humanist psychologist, proposed a hierarchy of five innate needs that activate and direct human behavior, and that we can find graphically in his pyramid of needs[33]:

1. Physiological
2. Security

---

[33] Maslow's Hierarchy of Needs. https://youtu.be/O-4ithG_07Q

3. Belonging and love
4. Esteem
5. Self-realization

Here are some considerations raised with respect to these needs:

- They are instinctive and hereditary. (Today, with the knowledge about neurosciences, we may begin to cast doubt on that statement.)
- The needs that Maslow mentions can be modified or canceled through learning, social expectations and fear of disapproval.
- Despite being born with these needs, the behaviors used to satisfy them are very varied.
- If a lower need is not satisfied at least partially, we will not be influenced by higher hierarchy needs.
- The lower the unmet need is, the greater the impulse to satisfy it.
- The dissatisfaction of a lower need produces a crisis in the individual, while a higher on does not. He called the first "deficit needs" and the second, "needs of growth or of being."

Pyramid proposed by Maslow

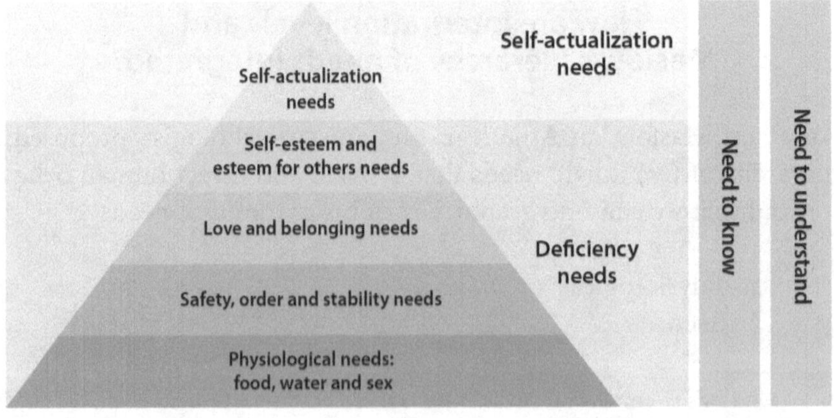

Additionally, he added other cognitive needs that exist outside the hierarchy raised by ensuring that knowing is stronger than understanding, so the need to know must be at least partially satisfied, before understanding can emerge.

Therefore, Maslow proposes that a person's behavior is determined by his innate motivational needs and by his way of perceiving reality, which is similar to Kelly's theory of constructs[34], which we mentioned earlier.

Both theories state, like the Enneagram, that a person's behavior is related to his or her perception of reality. Therefore, we can reach the following conclusion: the greater the perception of a person's helplessness, the less integrated their behavior will be, and they will expect the environment to provide them with what they consider they are unable to obtain by their own means. Personally, I find interesting coincidences between Maslow's Pyramid of Needs and the level of integration of the person.

Relationship between Maslow's proposal and the Enneagram integration levels

Rational mode matches Maslow's Self-Realization needs. In both cases, the person seeks transcendence and to improve the environment through their action.

They know themselves and their constructs, do not control them. They are so in contact with their essence and their human and spiritual potential that they do not depend on external validation in order to act. On the contrary, they have a strong need for spiritual development and selflessly help others. They are search for or have found their personal life mission.

Automatic mode is similar to the need for recognition or esteem proposed by Maslow, which is manifested in two ways:

---

[34] Described in the section: How the ego builds reality, (Chapter 4).

- Need for status and recognition – which, in turn, can be compared with the need of relatedness we referred to when talking about intelligence centers.
- Need to respect yourself.

Here we observe high levels of competence, independence and freedom. And although the person is in balance with the environment, it remains at a transactional level. Deliver a valuable product and expect some kind of recognition in return, whether its own or social.

Survival mode corresponds with the deficit needs identified by Maslow: food, safety and love. And being a deficit, the person will expect the environment to meet their needs.

Relationship between the hierarchy pyramid of Maslow's needs and the Enneagram metamodel

Rational mode

Self-realization needs

Automatic Pilot

Recognition needs

Membership needs

Survival Mode

Security needs

Physiological needs

According to this, the needs that have to do with survival correspond to the disintegrated levels of personality, where the environment is seen as a threat; that is why they feel justified in acting aggressively and even violently, to obtain that which will guarantee their survival. I think it is important to highlight that, more often than not, these needs are not really threatened, but it is rather the individual's perception that defines the situation.

People in this low consciousness level are not aware of what is going on around them; the story that prevails is their own. Their reticular activation system allows only the stimuli it considers adequate to uphold its construct, and, therefore, they do not realize that something is wrong. I think this factor is key to understand violence, bullying and other acts of human violence. If we do not transform our perception of danger, we will never vanquish violence and abuse. We have even reached the point where we think the human being is evil by nature. I firmly believe that human beings' greatest problem is that they live under constant threat and stress due to having lost contact with what makes them feel valuable: their essence. I have seen radical transformations in people again and again; once they are able to see that their essence holds all the answers and tools, they realize that they no longer need the world to save them, because they are the only ones who can do it. This empowering is what will actually transform our society. But it definitely begins with transforming ourselves as individuals.

In the end, everybody seeks wellness; the problem is the perspective from which they search for it. Every theory helps us reach that wellness from different perspectives but each of us needs to find our own path to leave fear behind and start living in love, and there are many ways of doing so.

CHAPTER 6

The Enneagram intelligences

The Enneagram proposes three intelligence centers: visceral (gut), emotional and mental. We all have the three centers, but we tend to distribute our energy in an unbalanced way, concentrating it on the center that we consider most useful for survival. It will be the perceptions of that center that we rely on to relate to the environment. The goal is to balance the energy through reconnecting all brain structures again.

Paul McLean, an American neurologist proposed a model that has served to explain the three intelligence centers proposed by the Enneagram. This model groups the brain functions into three systems or brains. Although neuroscience has proven that brain structures are not separated as he proposed, this model allows us to understand the brain functions easily.

The three brains

The differentiated structures according to McLean are:

- **Reptilian brain**: is the structure responsible for maintaining and regulating basic survival functions such as breathing and body temperature. It is made up of the basal ganglia, the brainstem and the cerebellum. This structure can be associated to the **gut center**.
- **Limbic brain**: it is the system responsible for generating action through emotions and motivation. Attraction to the pleasurable and evasion of the unpleasant.

  This system would be formed by the amygdala, the hypothalamus, the bark of the cingulum and the hippocampus. The limbic brain can be associated with the **emotional center**.

- **Modern brain or neocortex:** which is the most evolved and is responsible for advanced thinking, reasoning, speech, planning, abstraction and what we generally call higher functions. It is associated with the **mental center**.

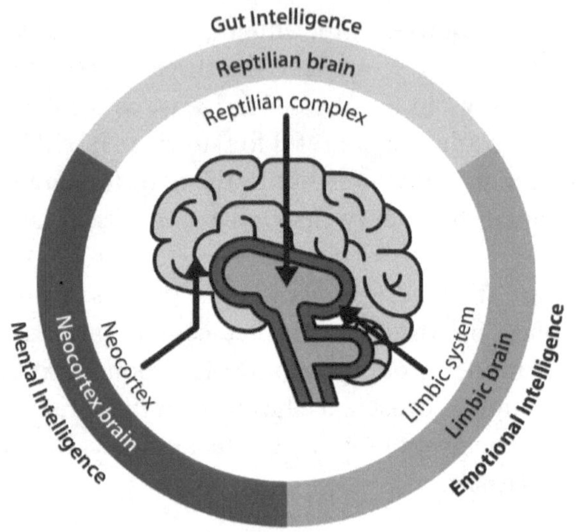

Intelligence centers

According to the theory of self-determination, all human beings have three basic psychological needs: the need for autonomy, the need for relatedness and the need to be competent; they are called basic because they are indispensable for the survival of the human being. These needs can explain the function of each center and thus help us understand the strategy that each personality uses to meet them.

Gut Center is governed by the **need for autonomy, it** refers to the individual's ability to make their own decisions and set limits. The emotion associated with this center is anger, which serves to set limits and defend the territory. The archaic fear associated with this need would be the fear of losing conquered territory. Each gut type satisfies the need for autonomy differently.

- Enneatype 8 - Seeks autonomy by controlling their environment.
- Enneatype 9 - Seeks autonomy by avoiding external control.
- Enneatype 1 - Seeks autonomy by controlling himself.

Heart Center is governed by the need for relatedness; that is the need to feel linked in two ways to the environment; that is, we need to feel sustained by it, while also need to feel that we have something to contribute. The emotion associated with this center is shame. This need seeks to compensate for the archaic fear of abandonment that occurs in offspring or mothers when they are raising offsprings. The self-esteem of these personalities depends largely on the response they get from others.

- Enneatype 2 - Looks for the link (create relatedness) through being loved and needed (contributes).
- Enneatype 3 - Looks for the link through generating admiration (contributes).
- Enneatype 4 - Looks for the link through generating sympathy (receives).

Head Center is governed by the **need for competence:** refers to the need for knowing that we have the necessary skills to get what we need to survive. The purpose of tribal initiation rites was for individuals to demonstrate their ability to survive on their own. The associated emotion is fear and responds to the archaic fear of not being able to obtain sustenance by their own means.

These personalities live in a state of permanent anxiety, thinking about the future to evaluate and deal with the possible scenarios that will arise.

- Enneatype 5 - Asserts competence by being the expert.
- Enneatype 6 - Seeks competence by detecting danger and threats. They focus on threats.

- Enneatype 7 - Seeks competence by planning for the future and anticipating solutions. They focus on obtaining resources while they are available.

Intelligence centers proposed by the Enneagram

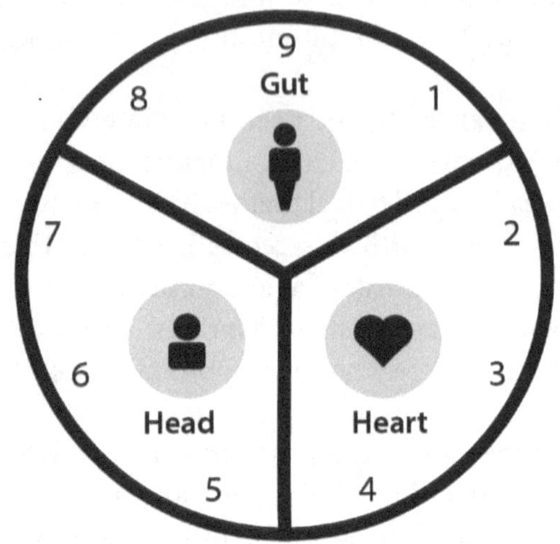

Based on this idea, we can conclude that fears determine that the individual's energy is concentrated in the center that he deems most necessary, which creates a specific brain structure to sustain it. Again, the concentration of energy is in response to a fear or need of the individual and is not the result of chance. This will be one of the first criteria for discrimination of inputs. Learning will be based on its usefulness to achieve this goal in order to survive.

It is a fact that personalities make decisions based on the perceptions of their center. However, if the ego is a survival mechanism, every personality is an automatic response on a somatic level, and the ego's procedure is the same for all of them. What varies is the input they use, and the type of response they give. What do I mean by all of this? Well, the brain is very simple, and nature works in a simple way. So, the biological process must be simple, despite the different Enneatypes. The brain receives an input through the ARAS, analyzes the input though the limbic brain system and then reacts in a certain way through the DRAS (Descendant Reticular Activation System) which works in the opposite direction to the RAS. That is, it generates an automatic response through the unconscious and automatic activation of certain parts of the brain, body, muscles, etc. Of course, we will have to do studies to conclusively prove this, but it is what I have observed over time in myself and the people I have trained.

On our radio show of August 22, 2016, KNOW YOURSELF, titled *"The brain: how it influences our personality"*, we interviewed Dr. Eduardo Calixto, a neuroscientific researcher from the *Universidad Nacional Autónoma de México* (UNAM). He explained the neurobiology of the Enneagram; here are some of the concepts he shared with us:

The amygdala regulates the individual's reactivity. People with low integration levels have a bigger and more reactive amygdala than people with a higher regular integration level. Another interesting point is that the amygdala has 13 different nuclei; some regulate emotions, and others visceral activity or instinctive responses. Another fact is that as the person has more neurons interconnecting the neocortex and the amygdala's nuclei, they will have more reasoned and fewer visceral reactions, due to the faster flow of information and the reduction of the amygdala's reactivity, causing its decreasing in size.

He mentioned that in order to pay attention to something, you must reduce the attention you give to other things. Basal ganglia filter information and only react in the moment your attention is grabbed.

The thalamus organizes information and decides what we pay attention to. This structure has pacemaker neurons which generate the frequency and attention cycles. As the thalamus and the prefrontal cortex are developed, brain filters decrease in number, and the person makes better decisions. By increasing connection speed between the neocortex and the amygdala, there will be a greater response control and less visceral reactivity. In a few words, what Calixto told us is that the lower the integration level, the greater the size of the amygdala. Additionally, the amygdala regulates the individual's automatic reactions (Survival mode).

With greater integration, the neocortex will regulate brain responses (Response mode) by sending inhibitory neurons towards the amygdala to prevent its reacting. To Calixto, it is clear that the greater the objectivity in perception, the less emotional reactivity will be present, and responses will be more rational and controlled.

What is next is investigating whether neurological and image studies match; our belief is that all Enneatypes' disintegrated reactions operate in the same way:

The reticular activating system in charge of perceiving stimuli will be specific to each intelligence center. For example, viscerals' ARAS will favor stimuli coming from the reptilian or primitive brain through skin perception. Emotional personalities will favor stimuli or inputs coming from the heart and smell receptors, while mentals' ARAS will favor and feed the amygdala with traditionally rational stimuli, such as sight, among others. There is a lot to do, but I think the Enneagram might be the lens that helps us design studies that make sense out of all the findings that have been made recently about the brain.

Likewise, the response type will be different in each Enneatype, and it will depend on the center being stimulated. For example, each Enneatype develops a specific somatic marker, but they all are automatic responses to received stimuli, and will be visceral, emotional or mental.

Each Enneatype will respond automatically and predictably to the stimuli it considers important to its survival. Oddly enough, these reactions correspond to the nine intelligences proposed by Elaine De Beauport and Aura Sofia Díaz, in their book *The Three Faces of the Mind*. They describe ten intelligence types the human being possesses, and, even though they were not familiar with the Enneagram when they proposed them, nine are descriptions of the Enneatypes' natural skills, and the tenth corresponds to intuition, which is perhaps the essence's natural intelligence.

This addition helps us understand better the type of strategy upon which each Enneatype is based. Every individual has access to all intelligences, but experiences during early childhood make children favor the use of a specific intelligence, forgetting or losing other skills as their ego, or personality, takes over. Each Enneatype builds a specific version of reality, which is upheld by the previously described selective attention mechanisms, and they react to the environment's threats in a specific way. The term "multiple intelligences" is widely questioned nowadays, which is why I will call them "strategic skills". What is interesting to me, is that each Enneatype identifies with one of the mentioned skills.

CHAPTER 7

The instincts that govern us

The instinctive variants

In the course of our evolution as human beings, we developed a set of three central instincts that are known in the Enneagram as instinctive variants[35] that will result in the Enneagram's 'subtypes'. These instincts are part of our body-based intelligence and the key to our biological imperatives. They are deeply ingrained in our unconscious nature and help in our survival as individuals and as a species.

Self-preservation instinct: The first instinct to evolve, self-preservation is an orientation towards survival, health and comfort. Of the three, it is the oldest. Animals are highly in tune with their self-preservation needs; they seek to ensure their own survival instead of looking at their group or partner to solve their problems and challenges. People with the dominant self-preservation variant can give up social

---

[35] "In contrast to this tendency to omit the notion of instinct in the interpretation of human behavior, the vision presented here does not only imply a theory of instinct (at least, it gives the instinct a third of the psychological field) , but coincides with the psychoanalytic notion of neurosis as a disturbance of instinct and, conversely, healing as a process of instinctive liberation. Unlike the two theories of Freud's instinct and Dollar and Miller's vision of behavior as a large multiplicity of impulses, the theory proposed here recognizes following the multiplicity of human motivation, three basic instincts and ends (leaving apart from purely spiritual motivation): survival, pleasure and relationship.

I think that although today some (such as gestaltists) would prefer to use cybernetic language and say that neurosis implies a disturbance of organismic self-regulation, few would question the great importance of the impulses of conservation, sexuality and relationship. , nor its joint central position as profound objectives of behavior. Although Freud's interpretation of human life put emphasis on the sexual impulse, Marx highlighted the momentum of conservation and current theorists of object relations highlight the momentum of relationship, I do not think anyone has adopted a vision that explicitly integrates these three fundamental impulses." (Naranjo, C., Character and Neurosis(Character and Neurosis), La Llave, 2012, p. 58).

position or the intensity of an experience in order to obtain physical well-being, security and other factors that ensure their own survival. They also manage their energy to keep it available to themselves.

Social instinct: Searches for membership and acceptance. The social instinct encourages people to get along with the group to be protected by it. It represents the need of the human being for social belonging. Those in whom the social variant predominates place greater importance on their relationships, on how they are seen by others and on being part of a group, that they may be able to forget their own needs for the sake of others. This variant also has to do with hierarchical levels and power within the group. These people have a light, adaptable and extended energy.

Sexual instinct: This instinct promotes the creation of lasting links with special people and, at the same time, seeks deep and authentic connections with them. This variant involves much more than simple procreation. People in whom the sexual instinct is predominant need to find meaning in all their relationships and feel passion, not only for others, but for work, art, sports or religion. They have a very focused and intense energy.

Modern humans are very far removed from our basic survival needs, to such a degree of confusing them with each other. This may be because as babies we are not independent: we cannot walk and we are not able to meet our own needs from birth. That is why our instincts do not manifest themselves in the same order as in animals and are modified by this latter circumstance.

From my point of view, the three instinctive variants are used in childhood as self-preservation mechanisms, favoring the one that gives us the best results. One of the conclusions Gurdjieff made was about the transformation of the lower instincts into higher instincts. I think he meant to recalibrate them precisely from an undistorted perspective of reality, to give them the purpose that nature designed. But this will only happen when we stop looking at ourselves from the perspective of the helplessness of childhood.

Instincts may have different ways of presenting themselves, depending on the energy we give each one. And again, this will depend on how useful we perceive them to be.

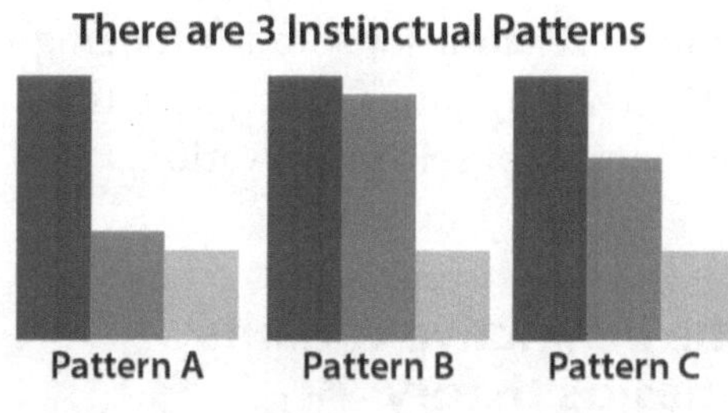

Note: we can find any instinctual combination. That is, any instinct may predominate and be present with any pattern.

A. The predominant instinct is highly developed, and the other two are not manifested.

B. There are two developed instincts, and the other one is not manifested.

C. There is an instinct manifesting intensely, the second one is less developed and the third one is not manifested.

The first instinct is the one to which we devote the most energy. It will manifest with greater force than our Enneatype[36], either for better or for worse. The second may be latent and generally does not cause us problems. The third is the least developed, though it is recommended that we pay attention to it, as it will help us integrate our personality.

If we look at the Enneatype as a survival mechanism, instinct must be responsible for an important part of the personality construct. Because the child must guarantee his survival, he will favor the strategy that has been most successful and, therefore, we will find three modifications of the self-preservation instinct that will be based on one of the following strategies:

- Accumulate and preserve the means of survival.
- Follow the rules of the clan to achieve their care through membership.
- Seek survival through generating deep ties with one or several protective figures.

---

[36] Vargas, A. (2018), *Eneagrama: El poder de los instintos. (Enneagram: The power of instincts)*, Alamah.

Thus, the three instincts are intertwined, although the one that provided the best results in childhood will show up more than the other two. That is, if generating deep links with the protective figures better guarantees self-preservation, the dominant instinct will be the sexual one. However, if having harmonious relationships and belonging to the group guarantees the care the child requires, it is likely that he favors the social instinct as a mechanism of self-preservation.

Justification of the instinctive variants from Damásio's theory

"The organizations are endowed since the birth of automatic survival mechanisms and acquire, through education and culture, a set of supplementary, desirable and socially acceptable strategies that allow them to make better decisions. These strategies increase their chances of survival, strongly improve their quality and provide the basis for the construction of the person. After birth, the human brain addresses postnatal development endowed with drives and instincts. On leaving childhood, he is provided with new survival strategies, which are closely related to those of the repertoire of instinctive responses."[37]

Maslow and the instinctive variants

The Enneagram states that, based on his primary experience, the baby concludes that by satisfying one of the three instincts, he will achieve total satisfaction of his needs. That is why some will develop more than another.

Imagine the conclusion that leads us to develop the predominance of one of the instincts:

---

[37] Damásio, A. (2011), *The error of Descartes (Descartes'Error: Emotion, Reason and the Human Brain)*, Andrés Bello, pp.167-168.

1. **Predominant self-preservation instinct:** the child learns that, if basic needs such as food, clothing, etc., are resolved, he will survive; for this reason, he will tend to seek his own welfare before those of others.
2. **Predominant social instinct:** the child concludes that being part of his tribe and gaining acceptance of his clan, his basic needs will be met by them. For people with this predominant instinct, acceptance of the other and compliance with social norms will be of utmost importance.
3. **Predominant sexual instinct:** the child will develop the strategy of achieving his survival through generating few, but very strong, connections with the people who can provide him with the basic sustenance.

This process of adaptation by the child not only means that his protective figures will meet his basic survival needs, but will be repeated in all the relationships he establishes throughout his life until he becomes aware of them. In practice, I have noted that the prevailing instinct difference causes more relational conflicts than the Enneatype itself.

As mentioned earlier, the Enneagram describes the modified instincts referred to by António Damásio, which also correspond to the three basic steps of the pyramid proposed by Maslow[38]. People's needs change depending on time, the situation, experience and when they comparing themselves with others.

From the Enneagram perspective, the three adapted instincts are hierarchically differentiated by each individual according to the environment in which they have developed.

The three basic survival instincts (self-preservation, social and sexual) have led humanity to where it is today. We know that in the human being, the three instincts intermingle and modify to increase the chances of survival and, moreover, they are modifiable through education, as Damásio mentions. So, it is logical to think that they will de-

---

[38] Schultz, D., Schultz, S. (2002), *Teorías de la personalidad (Theories of Personality)*, Ciudad de México: Cengage Learning, p. 303.

velop differently in each child, according to the environment in which he lived in early childhood. If we observe and accept that Maslow's Hierarchy of Needs does not work with total precision in the case of human beings, and that there are different instinctive patterns in all of us, we will understand why some of the deficiency needs proposed by Maslow are more important for some individuals than others.

With this consideration, we can say that Maslow's three deficiency needs are at the same level and the other two above, so we would obtain a pyramid that looks like this:

Relationship between Maslow's hierarchy of needs pyramid and the instinctive variants

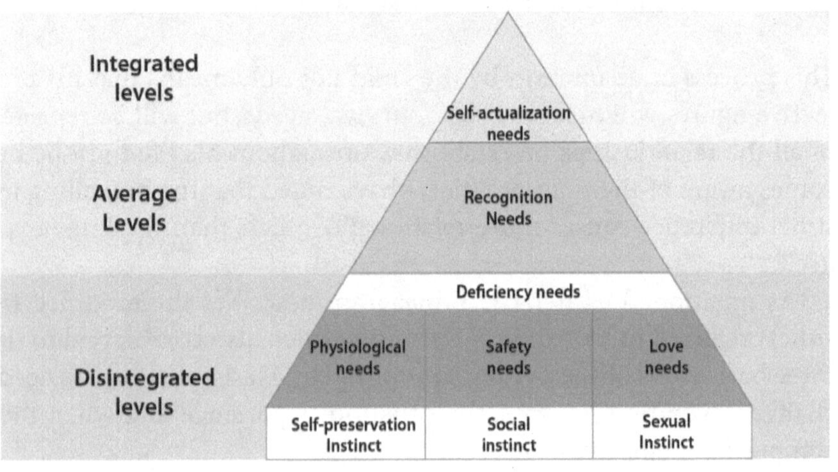

CHAPTER 8

Anatomy of the ego

How the ego behaves

The ego, or personality, can manifest itself in three ways, according to the level of threat perceived. As we have already seen, with greater helplessness, ego will overtake essence with the characteristic reactions of each Enneatype, while in situations of calm and security we will manifest the rational mode, which is governed by the essence or true being of the person.

Automatic mode: This describes the way each Enneatype behaves during normal situations. It is equivalent to the average integration level. In other words, it is the personality's "autopilot", and, it should be pointed out that it is where the greater percentage of the world population spends 90% of their time. These traits, far from being categorical, serve as an orientation for us to identify our Enneatype. The most important part of the Enneagram is to identify our somatic markers or automatic behaviors, since only in this way will the brain be able to update them.

Survival mode: This level describes the typical defense or attack reactions of each personality. That is, it describes the monster we all have inside, and that, when it awakens, takes over. Only by being aware of it will we be able to do something different when faced with the same circumstances. We should remember this monster is there to defend us from situations that are too much for us. The problem is that it behaves as if we were helpless kids in the face of external circumstances. Once we become aware, we will begin to have fun, observing those childish reactions, and thus being able to modify them.

Rational mode: Each personality responds in a characteristic way when it is in essence, that is, when it does not feel threatened and it is not necessary for the ego to defend it. We can say that in an ideal environment this is where we really are ourselves. Therefore, our inner monster is asleep and, if it manifests, it is so domesticated that it is our best friend, remembering that its function is to protect us and help us survive.

How the ego is created

The child's brain structures itself after birth to achieve its best adaptation to the environment in which the infant will live[39]. This is carried out through synaptic pruning and neuronal hyperconnectivity.

Even before birth, the child begins to adapt to the environment in which he will live. Today epigeneticists[40] — dedicated to the study of the mechanisms that regulate the expression of genes without a modification in the DNA sequence — are proving that possible childhood trauma causes alteration in the expression of genes in the brain, which can serve to explain certain behaviors in adults. In other words: it raises the possibility that brain structure is created to sustain the personality.

Personality, or ego, is not a response to the environment, but a strategy generated in response to the perception we have about our environment. Therefore, this strategy is unrealistic, but to us, it is the foundation of our reality.

Core construct

This is the conclusion from reality children draw, and it will be layer of reality upon which they will base all of their thoughts, feelings and actions. *"The world is like that"*. The construct sustains what the Enneagram describes as the basic survival belief. Let us remember that the neocortex is not fully developed before the second decade

---

[39] Comment made at the Workshop on mindfulness and cognitive therapy given by Dr. Pinos-Pey at the Intercontinental University of Mexico City, in May 2017.

[40] Carey, Nessa (2011). *The Epigenetic Revolution*, UK: Icon Books.

of life, so any frame of reference we might have created beforehand should be updated when our cognitive skills reach maturity.

Basic survival belief

In their search for survival, children reach the belief that, if they act in a certain way, their protective figures will provide the support they need to develop properly and to increase their possibilities of survival. *"To survive I must act in a certain way"*. This will produce mental fixation.

Mental fixation

This thought pattern will provoke cognitive distortion, which will lead to perception errors, which, in turn, will generate the development of mistaken ideas, thoughts and images. The brain seeks to pay attention to that which will help it satisfy its basic survival need; in order to achieve this, children develop a particular neurobiological and cognitive structure.

Neurobiological and cognitive structure

It is brain structure that allows individuals to adapt in order to survive. Through synaptic pruning and hyperconnectivity, they will develop scotomas, or blind spots, towards any situation that denies their core construct, and will develop selective attention towards that which, in their opinion, will provide a greater survival possibility. Each Enneatype seeks to satisfy its basic survival need, and, to achieve this, develops an alert system towards those inputs that are useful for survival, which is known as the ascendant reticular activation system (ARAS[41]). Another thing we must consider, which alters the perception of reality, is that when the brain recalls a memory, this memory becomes unstable, the same way a computer file does. When it is

---

[41] See Chapter 2 for a detailed explanation of the ARAS.

stored again, the last version of said memory is saved, that is, the updated version of the previous memory is saved. We add new feelings to the old memory each time we recall it, and that is why the more a story is told, the more it is twisted until it differs completely from the real event. This same characteristic is the one we use in the Enneagram to update responses and to modify the basic survival belief. By developing the inner observer, people realize painful memories or memories of danger are not painful or dangerous, and they can then modify the somatic markers of their personality.

The three ego variants

As a result of the evolutionary process, we have developed a set of three central instincts that are known in the Enneagram as instinctive variants and result in "subtypes[42]". These instincts are part of our visceral intelligence and seek to guarantee our survival as individuals and as a species. Therefore, in each Enneatype we will find the three versions:

- Self-preservation
- Social
- Sexual

What supports the ego structure

The ego wants our genes to reach the next generation, similar to what seeds do: when in an adverse environment, we have to enter a dormant phase and keep ourselves out of danger until circumstances are more favorable. This means we are kept in a comfort zone, and, of course, there is nothing more uncomfortable in life than the wrongly named comfort zone. I think it would be more appropriate to call it our safety zone. The thing is, that this structure is supported by the following mechanisms:

---

[42] Vargas, Andrea (2018), *Eneagrama, El Poder de los Instintos, (Enneagram, The power of Instincts)*, Alamah.

Scotomas: Our reticular activation system and attention filters leave out any information that may cause stress or discomfort, even though this implies our not being able to see opportunities or possible solutions, because our brain does not want us to move. These blind spots are the ones we must reduce by using the Enneagram, to broaden our consciousness and transform our life.

Selective attention: The ego develops a selective attention system towards those topics it deems essential for our survival. It is important to notice this in order to be able to modify it.

Defense mechanisms: This is a confusing topic for those of us who are not psychologists, and there is a great diversity of opinions about them. Ginger Lapid-Bogda[43], a North American world leader in the Enneagram, describes the mechanisms proposed by Claudio Naranjo:

Defense mechanisms are the unconscious psychological strategies we use to deal with difficult situations as a way to reduce our anxiety, sadness, or anger and maintain our self-concept, and they appear when we are avoiding something especially important for our development. Because each Enneagram type uses a certain defense mechanism more than the others, they become quite proficient at using it even though these old and often outdated psychological mechanisms may cause more harm than good.

From the neuroscientific point of view, I believe they are the result of the brain structure developed by each Enneatype.

How the ego thinks

The ego, or personality, emerges as a child's strategy to adapt to an environment that he does not understand and cannot modify due to his helplessness. Given that fear we call basic, the child develops strat-

---

[43] Lapid-Bogda, Ginger (2019), Enneagram Learning portal. www.theenneagraminbusiness.com

egies that allow him to survive. Each Enneatype will display different strategies and behaviors that are generated by their basic fear.

The good thing is that each personality will also develop a certain set of skills or abilities that no other Enneatype has, resulting in natural talents.

Basic fear

This fear arises as a result of the conclusion the child drew about the environment that surrounded it during the first years of its life, and they decided that it would be what would keep them alive for the rest of their days. It is precisely this fear we must modify. But, since it is so ancient and deep, it is not obviously apparent. Identifying it begins with determining their Enneatype and by observing themselves until they are able to pinpoint this fear and work with it.

Cognitive error

This is the premise from which an individual decides what information is useful and what is not. Let us say it is the lens used to filter everything around us. It may have been useful and adequate when it was created in childhood, but perhaps now it is time to update it.

Motivation

It describes what induces each Enneatype to act in its characteristic manner, and it is closely related to the basic belief of **survival**.

Multiple intelligence[44] or strategic skill

They are natural skills that allow the human being to survive and develop. Every individual has access to all intelligences, but the first childhood experiences make the child favor the use of a certain skill, forgetting or ignoring the other intelligences as their ego structures itself. The term "multiple intelligences" is being questioned today, and I think it would be more correct to call them "strategic skills." Knowing them can help us better understand each ego's cognitive process.

Basic intelligence gives the human the ability to approach and to move away correctly from a situation. It is the impulse to act. One of its special uses is to open up ways to explore the unknown. **It corresponds to Enneatype 8.**

Pattern intelligence. The pattern comprising the organization of energy in the reptilian brain has a stabilizing or harmonizing function, and may be where resistance to change comes from. **It corresponds to Enneatype 9.**

Parameter intelligence, or the ability to establish time, space, field of action or thought boundaries. Rigid parameters may produce perfectionism and inflexibility. Proper direction allows for the establishment of new parameters, to open up to more alternatives. **It corresponds to Enneatype 1.**

Affective intelligence provides the ability to affect and be affected by people, things or situations. **It corresponds to Enneatype 2.**

Motivational or "want" intelligence. It is the ability to want something, and to follow the impulse to chase it until we get it. **It corresponds to Enneatype 3.**

---

[44] Beauport, E. y Díaz, A. (2008), *Las tres caras de la mente. El desarrollo de las inteligencias mentales, emocionales y del comportamiento (The Three Faces of Mind: Developing Your Mental, Emotional, and Behavioral Intelligences)*. 1ª ed., Caracas, Venezuela: Alfa Grupo Editorial.

Emotional or mood intelligence. This intelligence allows us to "listen" to information-laden emotions, to be able to live within them and to leave them when appropriate. It is to the limbic brain what rational intelligence is to the neocortex. **It corresponds to Enneatype 4.**

Rational intelligence is responsible for logical and analytical sequential thought, as well as for cause-and-effect thought. **It corresponds to Enneatype 5.**

Associative or random connections intelligence is the ability to associate or relate to that with which you want to associate. Its difficulty would reside in not being able to reach a decision or conclusion. **It corresponds to Enneatype 6.**

Spatial, visual and auditory intelligence. This is the mental ability to visualize something better for the future. Some of its uses are planning and entertaining. **It corresponds to Enneatype 7.**

Intuitive intelligence, which also corresponds to the right hemisphere of the neocortical brain, does not bear a correspondence with the typologies described by the Enneagram. This intelligence, whose ability is to know directly from within, derived from a non-thinking mental state, in my opinion, is a quality of the essence that manifests when one is on an advanced integration path. In other words, when one has attained the ability to use all other intelligences properly, one experiences a perfect inner unity.

How to change the cognitive pattern

While we are advancing in self-control - the knowledge of ourselves - the defense mechanisms deactivate and we integrate the characteristics we used to deny in us. That is, as we become aware of the mental constructs that underpin our ego, we can modify them in a natural way to incorporate more response possibilities and thus stop acting in a reactive way. This transformation happens because the scotomas created to maintain a frame of reference that worked in the first years of life start dissolving. The behavioral patterns characteristic of the low integration levels of our Enneatype are modified because we discover that we have many more response options than those that were useful in our early childhood.

The Enneagram is a map of human behavior that generates self-knowledge and, therefore, contact with the spiritual part of the human being, also known as the true self, to stop living in what is known as a false self or ego.

We begin to stop identifying with the ego by introducing the vision that within us that there is already something unique and irreplaceable, which is our essence. Returning to Dan Siegel and the neuroscientific facts, we can say that the Enneagram describes the way we act when we are in **reaction mode**.

CHAPTER IX

Neuroscience of personalities

We have talked throughout this book about the different theories of Enneagram and its relation to many neuroscientific concepts; now we will see how they all apply to each Enneatype or personality.

Getting to know each other better allows us to relate in a healthier way with the people around us. By understanding the reasons why others act in a certain way, we can understand them better and find new forms of relationship. It also provides us with a valuable tool when it comes to educating our children.

One: The Reformer

Idealist, ethical, structured, thorough

They live by their moral principles and their ideals. They have a very clear idea of what is right and what is wrong. They seek to improve the world and have very high goals. Integrity, honesty, truth and justice are very important to them. They can be very critical and have an internal judge that watches over them constantly.

Characteristic behaviors

Automatic mode

They are idealistic, ethical, responsible and hard-working. They live by their moral principles and their ideals. They have a very clear idea of what is right and what is wrong. They seek to improve the world, they have very high standards, and tend to be impatient with human failure. Integrity, honesty, truth and justice are very important to them.

They are very hard on themselves and others. They have a compulsive need to correct mistakes. They say "I should" and "I have to" a lot. They are convinced that there is only one correct way of doing things, and they seek perfection in everything they do, which is why almost always results do not meet their expectations. They are afraid to make mistakes, since they feel they will be criticized or judged. They can be harsh, impatient, judgmental and emotionally reserved.

Survival mode

In more threatening circumstances they become intolerant and do not accept any type of negotiation. They can be dogmatic, inflexible, severe in their judgment, too serious, obsessive-compulsive, controlling, anxious and jealous.

Rational mode

They are connected to their true self and are capable of perceiving the world as perfect; therefore, they accept reality with serenity. The world is perfect, and everything fulfills the purpose for which it was created. *"My attention will be focused on seeing what I can learn from each situation life puts forth. Because I know that everything that happens is perfect, for the universal good."*

How ego is formed

Ones perceive that their environment is not ideal; it ceases to be safe and nutritious and becomes a threat to their survival. They begin to perceive that their needs are not met how and when they arise. They think: *"They do not feed me when I am hungry". "They do not cover me when I am cold"*, etc. *"Therefore, I feel responsible for transforming it into what it should be, into what it was when I was in the womb."*

In their helplessness, children try to adapt to a hostile and scarcely nutritious environment. This makes *Ones* form an image of themselves as being bad or imperfect. Additionally, since they depend on their parents or protective figures to survive, they will draw the conclusion that since they are imperfect, they are not loved, and if they are not loved, they will not get the care they need, which biologically means death. In order to survive, they will have to develop strategies that allow them to be good and to correct wickedness in themselves and the world. Their attention will be focused on correcting imperfection. Their vision or construction of the world will be the consequence of how they look at it.

Core construct: "The world is an imperfect place"

Oscar Ichazo presented the concept of Holy Ideas, and *Ones'* would be Holy Perfection[45]. The Healthy view of *Ones* is the ability to see perfection in everything that happens, despite its not fitting their concept of "good". Let us set an example: Painful situations are difficult, yet perfect, because they bring out the best in human beings. I do not mean to say they are desirable, but once they happen, one can choose to complain and resist or learn. If we look at this type of situations in our life, we notice that we have learned the most from them. The ability to see an aspect of reality without distortion or judgment is what I call healthy view, and, to my understanding, it is the equivalent to Ichazo's Holy Ideas.

In essence, *Ones* can perceive "Perfection" in everything that happens, and in the world in general. The virtue of Serenity arises in them, since they accept reality as something that is the result of a greater plan.

---

[45] In the business world, these terms are not well received, that is why I call them "healthy view of the world".

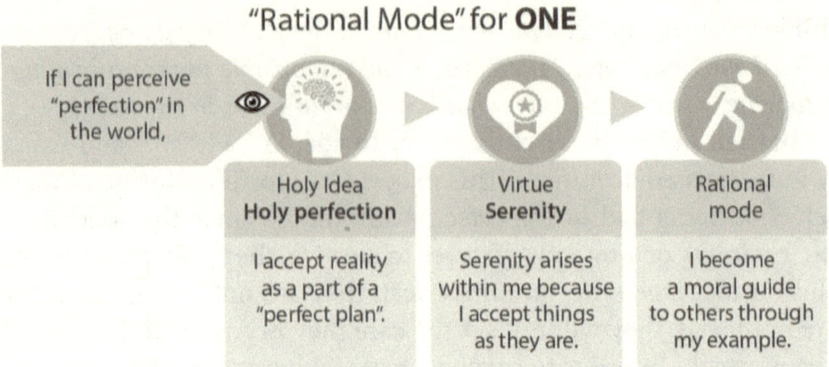

When *Ones* move away from their essence due to the typical fear of their Enneatype, their vision becomes distorted and they begin to seek the way of satisfying their need to find perfection. Instead of looking for it in what already is, they move away from their essence, from the Universe, from God; and choose to produce it instead of changing their view or reference point. This breaking point with their true self is what is described in some traditions as "loss of paradise". The greater their focus on improvement, the greater their distortion of reality. Let us remember that the brain needs to solve to avoid stress, and it does not seek the truth, but survival. The way in which they solve the issue is known in the Enneagram as mental fixation, and each Enneatype has a typical mental fixation. *Ones'* fixate on wanting to perfect themselves and the world around them. The more obsessed they are with correcting the mistake, the more they will disintegrate.

Mental fixation of Ones: "I have to be perfect and I have to make the world around me better"

This fixation of seeking perfection and telling others how they should act, according to their own perfection scheme, angers them when other people do not do what *Ones* think is right according to their individual parameters and concepts of perfection. Anger arises, which is the passion that will drive them to act. Their inner child thinks: "I am so good. However, the rest..."

This strategy will manifest, as in every Enneatype, through one of the three instincts, which in the case of *Ones* are:

- Preservation instinct: To improve oneself.
- Social instinct: To improve the world.
- Sexual instinct: To improve those close to them.

Depending on the environment or family where they were born, they will develop one need more that the other.

How is the ego structure upheld?

Ones' ego maintains itself through the following mechanisms:

- Scotoma: Towards their imperfection and flaws.
- Selective attention: Towards mistakes in order to correct them.
- Defense mechanism: Reaction Formation

Reaction Formation[46] is used by *Ones* to reduce or eliminate anxiety created from their own thoughts, feelings, or behaviors that they con-

---

[46] Lapid-Bogda, Ginger (2019), Enneagram Learning portal. www.theenneagraminbusiness.com

sider unacceptable by responding in the exact opposite of their real reaction. The *One's* active inner critic dictates what is acceptable based on social mores, contextual expectations, and moral principles, and reaction formation becomes a defensive remedy when the *One* has what he or she deems unacceptable reactions.

An interesting aspect of reaction formation is that at one level, it is unconscious and automatic. At another level, however, *Ones* usually know that this behavior is the opposite of the real truth, but this realization usually happens after the fact rather than while it is occurring. In addition, and perhaps surprisingly, *Ones* who acknowledge that they've behaved in a way diametrically opposed to their true feelings, thoughts, and desires rarely exhibit embarrassment or negative self-judgments about having done so.

How do *Ones* think?

Basic fear
Fear of being wicked, corrupt or defective.

Cognitive error
Ones think that if they are not perfect, they will not be cared for and have their needs attended to, so they constantly seek to be and prove that they are good. To do this, they use constant comparison with others as a parameter.

Motivation
Achieving excellence.

Strategic skill of *Ones*

The developed skill, according to Elaine De Beauport's[47] theory, is **pa-**

---

[47] Beauport, E. y Díaz, A. (2008), *Las tres caras de la mente. El desarrollo de las inteligencias mentales, emocionales y del comportamiento (The Three Faces of Mind: Developing Your Mental, Emotional, and Behavioral Intelligences)*, 1ª ed., Caracas, Venezuela: Alfa Grupo Editorial.

rameter intelligence, or the ability to establish time, space, fields of action or thought.

> *Parameter Intelligence enables us to guide our energy. Otherwise, we would not know what to do with the constant and abundant flow of energy that penetrates our reptilian brain. Parameters work as a margin or limit, they are the boundary that guides our energy. At first, we took these parameters from our environment, they reached us via our formation. You use certain beliefs as your parameters, which have been valued in your family for generations, and you call them values. Your values provide a constant reference so you do not have to constantly think of each circumstance that arises...Parameters help and also damage...Old limits neither die nor disappear, they merely become ineffective. More often than not, we wait for a crisis in order to change, instead of being on the alert and reviewing values, routines and habits, constantly updating them. (pp. 323-325)*

Parameters are a group of limitations that produce certain behaviors, and that provide stability. These can be religious, social, personal, physical or time-related. For example, drinking coffee every morning is a temporary parameter, because it always happens at the same time, and chemical, because it provides caffeine to the body. Not having coffee in the morning will cause an unbalance in the body which will trigger stress, tension and even panic.

Parameters generate routines, which become habits when they become essential to us. When we talk about chemical parameters, the routine is called addiction. That is why it is so difficult to quit habits and addictions, since the body demands to live within the parameters that provide it with safety. In other words, keeping ourselves within our parameters implies biological survival; to step out from them is a risk of death for the reptilian brain. Parameters allow us to act automatically without our having to analyze and constantly decide where to direct our energy.

The ego, whose goal is survival, will put up plenty of resistance to changing *Ones'* parameters, and in addition, it will provoke anger when any of

Ones' survival parameters are affected. That is why *Ones* feel the owners of the truth, because they think that they have to stay within their parameters in order to survive. That is why neither the Enneatype's typical behavior nor their reality construct will be modifiable, until they do not prove to themselves, based on reality, that said construct is not valid. The moment *Ones* feel safer and allow themselves to analyze their core construct with the neocortex, they will update it spontaneously. But while the perception is of danger or insecurity, survival mode will remain activated, and it will not be possible to modify the core construct on which the whole personality mechanism is based. In other words, they will be in reaction mode, they will have a fixed mentality and they will seek to be right at all costs.

Rigid parameters give rise to perfectionism and inflexibility. Proper guidance allows people to establish new parameters, to open to other alternatives. Since this ability to stay within acceptable parameters makes the individual feel safe, the more threatened *Ones* feel, the more rigid those parameters will be.

The brain can cheat and distort reality just so the individual survives. As *Ones* move down the integration levels, they seek to feel good and perfect, even though it does not have anything to do with reality. The more the level of consciousness decreases, the greater scotoma towards their imperfection and a greater attention to others' flaws to justify themselves. Instead of making a better world, or of doing what needs to be done, they do what makes them feel good.

They might not necessary do things to make the world better, rather things that make them feel like they are good, such as exercising, washing dishes, washing cars, etc. Through these activities they reduce the stress of feeling defective, but they are not necessarily the ones that will lead them to fulfill their ideal of making a better world, since they are not based on real needs, rather on the ego's particular needs.

The less their ability to perceive reality, the less efficient their responses and behavior will be, and the more dissatisfaction they will feel.

How to change the cognitive pattern of *Ones*

The only way to modify parameters is through a conscious analysis of their effectiveness. In other words, parameters have to be updated to the needs of their current reality. As in all cases, the brain will always pick what it thinks is the most adequate to survive. *Ones* must learn to accept themselves as being imperfect, and to understand that they are not any less valuable for it. To the extent that they are able to accept themselves, they will be able to accept others, and they will be less severe.

Tips to improve if you are a *One*

- Look for what can be better, instead of paying attention to what is wrong.
- Open up and accept that there are different ways of doing things.
- Forgive imperfection in yourself and in others.
- Motivate others by being more sensitive and generous with praise.
- Take time off to play sports, rest and have fun.
- See how others are more flexible and are not as severe as yourself.
- Note that when you feel bad about yourself, you start looking for someone who is worse than you to justify yourself.
- When you perceive anger in you, ask yourself: Am I doing what I want or what I should?

Two: The Collaborator

Obliging, attentive, compassionate, generous

They easily recognize needs in others, and prefer giving to receiving. They are warm, good confidants and they are generous with their time. They seek to be loved, needed and indispensable to other people. They may become manipulative in order to reach their goals.

Characteristic behaviors

Automatic mode

They seek to be needed, loved and appreciated, to become indispensable to others. Their emotional life is really important. They relate easily to others. People and relationships are the most important things to them. They are seductive, looking constantly for others to like them. They easily recognize needs in others, and are always ready to give advice or to render a service. They sacrifice too much in order to be appreciated. They may give help when it is not needed, which makes them intrusive and inappropriate.

Survival mode

In more threatening circumstances, they become hysterical and ambitious, and they may manipulate until they satisfy their needs. They can get possessive, sickly-sweet, hypocritical, self-interested and they may play the martyr.

Rational mode

They are generous with their time and their feelings. They greatly empathize with others. They give for the sheer pleasure of giving, expecting nothing in return. Their giving is unselfish. They are warm and good confidants. They know their needs and how to express them. They are connected to their true self, and they are capable of perceiving the world as a loving and unconditional place. Therefore, they know themselves to be worthy of love, and they humbly respond to the ultimate reality. Love is available for those who want to receive it. *"My attention will be fixed on seeing in which ways I am held by the Universe, and on sharing the love I freely receive with others."*

How ego is formed

It begins when the child perceives that the environment is not ideal and stops being safe and nurturing and begins to be a threat to their safety. *Twos* begin to realize that love is conditional and that it is not good to meet their own needs before those of others, therefore, they arrive to the following conclusion: *"If I do not give love, I will not be loved; and if I'm not loved, I will not receive the care I need, and I will die. I have to get them to love me."*

They realize that they can manipulate the environment through raising responses of love towards themselves. Therefore, they begin to develop special attention to the needs of others and meet them as a way to ensure that later, they will get the care they need to survive.

They form an image of themselves as generators and responsible for the well-being of others. In order to survive they will have to develop strategies that allow them to make others want and need them. Their attention will be focused on issues that have to do with the needs of others. And their image of the world will be a consequence of this distorted perception of the world.

Core construct: In this world you have to give in order to receive

Oscar Ichazo presented the concept of Holy Ideas, and *Twos* would be Holy Freedom[48]. The Healthy View of *Twos* is the ability to know that Good happens even if we choose not to do it. In order to see this, we require the humility of knowing ourselves to be mere channels of Good in the world. Being aware of that healthy freedom, when they choose to help, *Twos* expect nothing in return. The Healthy view is the ability to see an aspect of reality without distortion or judgement, and, to my understanding, it is the equivalent to Ichazo's Holy Ideas.

In essence, Twos are able to perceive "goodness" in the world, without having to produce it. That is why they are humble, by knowing Good happens in a lot of ways and that they do not need to do anything to be loved.

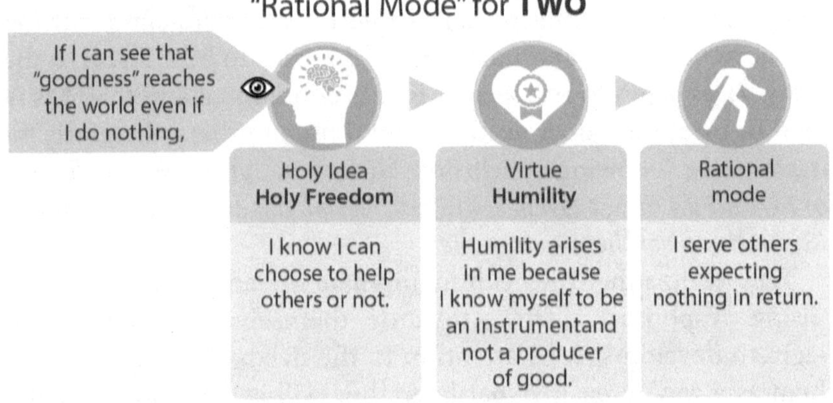

When *Twos* disconnect from their essence, they begin to perceive the need to feel loved. Instead of going back to their true self, in order to contact their own love, they start to produce a loving response in others. This breaking point with their essence is what is described in some traditions as "loss of paradise". *Twos* begin to

---

[48] In the business world, these terms are not well received, that is why I call them "healthy view of the world".

fixate on wanting to gain love by loving others. The greater their fixation on earning love, the greater their disintegration and distortion of reality. Thinking that, if they satisfy others' needs, they are cared for and protected. They will seek to feel good by generating well-being around them.

Remember that the brain seeks to survive and needs to solve the problem to reduce stress and cortisol release. The way in which *Twos* solve it is known in the Enneagram as their mental fixation. Each Enneatype has its own mental fixation.

Mental fixation: "I have to produce well-being for the world around me"

This fixation of selectively solving others needs and not paying attention to their own, generates a sense of superiority. Pride arises, which is the passion that will drives them to act. The inner child thinks: *"Look, mom, how nice I am."*

"Survival mode" for **TWO**

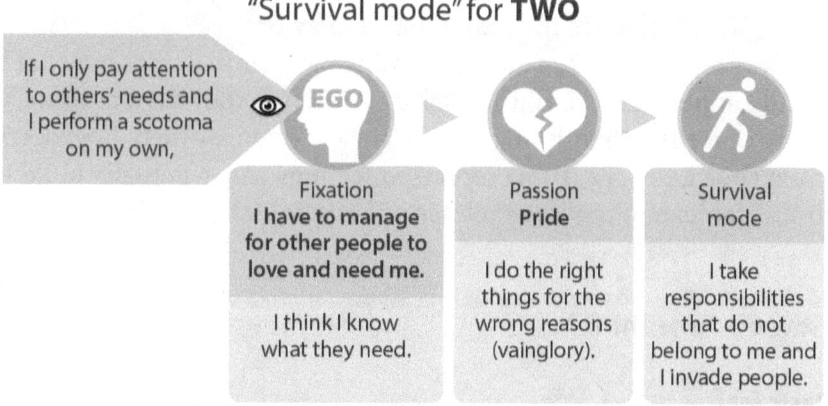

This strategy will manifest, as in all Enneatypes, through one of the three instincts, which in the case of *Twos* will be:

- Preservation instinct: They satisfy their needs by playing the role of "helpless" so others take care of them.

- Social Instinct: They satisfy their needs through their cunning and weaving social networks.
- Sexual Instinct: They satisfy their needs through seduction and conquest.

How is the ego structure upheld?

Ego upholds itself through the following mechanisms:
- Scotoma: Towards their own needs.
- Selective attention: Towards the needs of others in order to satisfy them.
- Defense mechanism: Repression

Repression[49] occurs when *Twos* hide information about themselves – feelings, desires, wishes, aversions, fears, and needs that are too difficult to acknowledge consciously – from themselves. However, the repressed information does not disappear; instead, expression of the information is controlled or suppressed, although it continues to unconsciously influence the individual's behavior.

Twos repress so often and so readily that their reactions may not be readily apparent, even to themselves. Although they may, at times, be aware of feeling slightly angry, they are less often aware of how deeply upset they truly are. These repressed feelings can eventually build up to such an extent that they release an eruption of feelings.

How do *Twos* think?

Basic fear
They are afraid of not being loved due to their being unworthy of love.

---

[49] Lapid-Bogda, Ginger (2019), Enneagram Learning portal. www.theenneagraminbusiness.com

Cognitive error

Twos think that to get attention and care, they must first satisfy the needs of others, which wears them out and leads them to always have a hidden unconscious agenda.

Motivation

Serving others in order to feel loved and needed.

Strategic skill of *Twos*

The skill they develop, according to Elaine De Beauport's[50] theory, is **affective intelligence of the limbic brain**, which refers to the ability of letting oneself be affected by people, ideas, objects or expressions.

> *This Intelligence implies letting oneself be affected by someone or something. It means having the ability to feel deeply, to feel moved. Affective Intelligence is the process through which we choose to be affected or not, and in what measure. This intelligence allows us to consciously begin the process of feeling and to unconsciously inhibit it. Emotions control our internal organs, and that is why it is important to let ourselves feel and be affected in order to expand and contract our organs. This intelligence, when it is used well, allows us to select the events by which we will let ourselves be affected, instead of being victims of external circumstances. (pp. 147-148)*

The neocortex is the gateway to the secondary emotions. Depending on what we think will happen, we allow ourselves to feel emotions or not. When we are not aware of our negative feelings, they trigger constrictive vibrations in our organs, until a physical reaction of illness or a psychological crisis takes place. Affective intelligence is key to their inner life's relation to the rest of the world. Just as we think and feel

---

[50] Beauport, E. y Díaz, A. (2008), *Las tres caras de la mente. El desarrollo de las inteligencias mentales, emocionales y del comportamiento (The Three Faces of Mind: Developing Your Mental, Emotional, and Behavioral Intelligences)*, 1ª ed., Caracas, Venezuela: Alfa Grupo Editorial.

in relation to the rest of the world, we also have emotional responses towards it. Nobody teaches us to relate emotionally to the world, we simply let ourselves be affected by it, and we try to control our emotional reactions by thinking, sensing or acting with our reptilian brain.

In their search to feel good and generous, *Twos* sense the needs of others; and, without thought or analysis, throw themselves wholly into satisfying them. This lack of reflection and analysis to detect whether the other's needs are real, or whether the other person actually wants the help they feel they need, makes them invasive sometimes, and makes them act automatically in order to satisfy their own need to feel useful. Another thing to consider is that the neocortex blocks any need *Twos* may feel, since they have the belief that having needs will turn them into a selfish person. That is why *Twos* with low levels of self-mastery have no connection to their emotions and can be histrionic. In other words, they act the emotions they think they should be feeling, and are perceived as insincere by others.

Just like Enneatype *Ones*, as *Twos* descend through the integration levels, they will act to feel generous, even if it has nothing to do with the other person's real needs. As the level of consciousness decreases, there will be a greater scotoma towards their needs and greater attention to others' needs in order to satisfy them. Therefore, their interest will be further and further apart from others' well-being, and they will be more focused on satisfying their unconscious needs to feel generous and useful to others.

How to change the cognitive pattern of *Twos*

A formula that is highly useful for people with Enneatype *Two*, is that before going on a crusade for help, they should ask themselves the following questions:

1. Do I want to? Analyze whether it is a product of my Ego and of my belief that the world needs me to keep spinning.
2. Can I help? Analyze whether I can actually help, if I will not be going against my needs by doing it.

3. Must I rescue? Think whether the person I wish to help will actually be benefited by it, or if, on the contrary, I will be generating codependence to myself.

Tips to improve if you are a *Two*

- Use mind as much as the heart.
- Learn to retire, not to save and get involved in things that don't correspond to you.
- Openly ask for what you need, instead of manipulating or flattering.
- Wait for others to ask for help or advice and don't throw yourself on the helping crusade as usual.
- Learn to say NO and set limits.
- Remember that, in cases of emergency on airplanes, you have to put on your oxygen mask first and then help others.

Three: The Executor

Competent, self-confident, successful, ambitious

They focus their energy on reaching their goals and are very skilled at adapting to any situation. They seek to earn admiration and prestige. They are always in a hurry; slow people get on their nerves. They see themselves as winners, and they give a lot of importance to this image, as well as to the opinions of others. They may be workaholics as well as highly competitive.

Characteristic behaviors

Automatic mode

They are efficient, confident and their self-esteem is real. They possess great skill to adapt to any situation. They are organized, independent, committed; they always have a goal to achieve. Being workaholics, they have a lot of energy and they are very competitive. They are masters of disguise. They care more about form than substance. They confuse their true self with the identity that their activity or work gives them. They are in great need to be recognized. Their goal is to achieve success and prestige. They give a lot of importance to their "winner" image and to others' opinion.

Survival mode

In more threatening circumstances, they do not have access to feelings or intimacy. They are arrogant, opportunistic. They use any ruse they can think of just to stay at the top. They can be deceitful, conceited and superficial.

Rational mode

They are connected to their true self, and they are able to perceive themselves as valuable. They are interested in developing themselves as a person in all aspects of their life. They know themselves and they are in contact with their real feelings and their vulnerability. They are leaders capable of motivating and inspiring others through their excellence. Therefore, they are authentic and confident. *"I am valuable and I do not need to do anything to prove it. My attention will be fixed on seeing how I can empower others. If I am aware of my value, I do not need to please or impress others. I can be myself, and act from the freedom of authenticity".* Their attention will be on helping others find their true personal value.

How ego is formed

From an early age, *Three* children concluded that they needed to do things to gain the acceptance of others, and therefore, their attention will be on perceiving what is valuable for the world and developing it in them. They become the satisfiers of the unspoken desires of the family, and unconsciously postpone their own: *"I put aside my emotions, because my motivation will be to be successful so that they give me the approval that I feel I don't deserve."*

In their helplessness, *Threes* try to adapt to a hostile and non-nurturing environment. They start looking for constant recognition and sacrifice a lot in order to receive it. This behavior is reinforced with phrases such as: "Great, that's my son! Only the first place is worth it!" Or constant comparisons with other children.

From an early age, they know how to tune into the wishes and expectations of others and learn to use their childhood intuition to please others and generate smiles of approval. This pattern learned in the first years will be what governs their life. The belief is: "I have to be successful to be loved." They will repeat the pattern automatically with all their relationships throughout their life, generating in them an emptiness and dissatisfaction impossible to fulfill with any achievement.

The cognitive error lies in believing that their personal value is in the achievements or in the applause and not in their personal worth.

The greater the stress, the more they need that external approval. Their attention will be focused on issues that have to do with success and the achievement of goals and results. Their vision of the world will be a consequence of this distorted perception of him.

Core construct: In this world you have to be successful in order to survive

Oscar Ichazo presented the concept of Holy Ideas, and *Threes* would be Holy Law[51]. Their healthy view is the ability to see that, in the universe, everything is displayed in a constant and harmonious manner, and that anything we do will have repercussions for others. We can make reference to the theory of homeostasis, which is the search for balance in the universe, and to the fact that we can notice it from cellular level to universal level. That is why, when they are in contact with their essence, they have the ability to see balance and harmony in everything that happens. The ability to look at an aspect of reality without distortion or judgement is what I call healthy view, and, to my understanding, it is the equivalent to Ichazo's Holy Ideas.

Threes, knowing themselves to be valuable for being part of the whole, and for the simple fact of being part of that perfect plan, accept themselves to be valuable, and allow themselves to be authentic.

"Rational Mode" for THREE

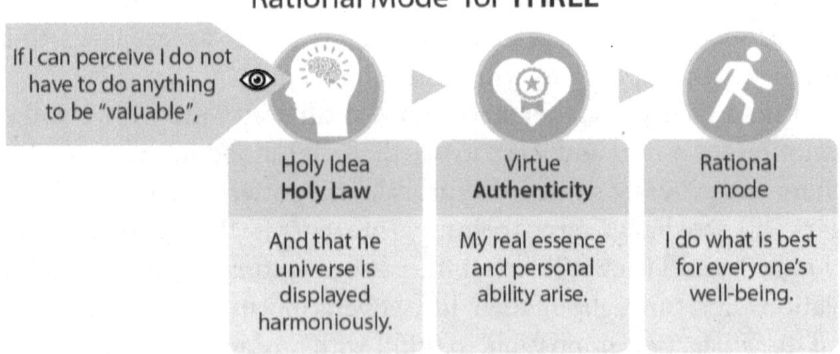

---

[51] In the business world, these terms are not well received, that is why I call them "healthy view of the world".

When *Threes* disconnect from their true self, they begin to feel the need to recover their feeling of personal worth, but instead of going back to their essence, they start doing things in order to feel valuable. They lose the awareness of being united to the whole, and they begin to look for success without thinking of others or of the consequences. *Threes* fixate on wanting to produce their feeling of worth by achieving admiration and prestige. The greater their fixation on being valuable, the more they will disintegrate. *Threes* start fixating on their goals, and on standing out in what they think will make them feel valuable. Since they were children, they learned that they must succeed in order to be recognized, and they will mistake love for recognition. *"I have the desire to find my personal value, but instead of contacting my essence for it, I begin to seek acceptance and external applause to feel valuable."*

Mental fixation: "I have to achieve my goals and be successful to feel valuable"

This strategy of looking for external recognition to feel valuable gives rise to vanity, since for *Threes*, it is no longer about feeling valuable, it is rather about generating an image of worth in others. In order to accomplish this, they will need to highlight their achievements for others to notice them. If we think of a child, the childish behavior of saying *"Look mom, I am so good at this!"* is fixated.

"Survival mode" for **THREE**

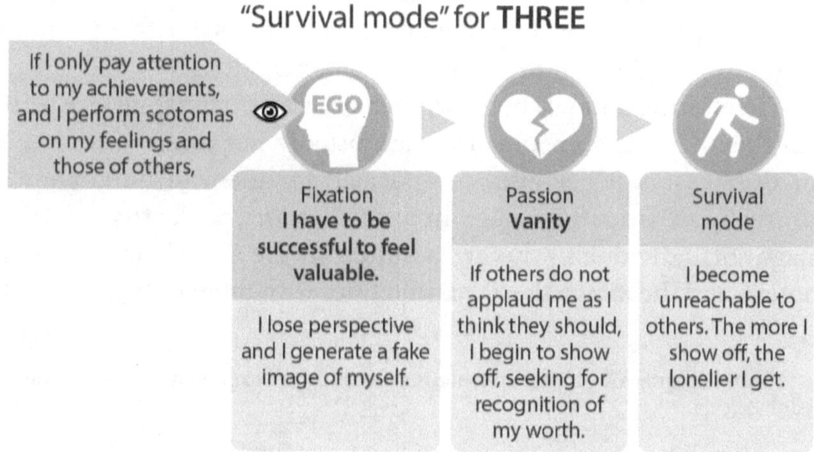

This strategy will manifest, as in all Enneatypes, through one of the three instincts, which in the case of *Threes* are:

- Preservation instinct: Feeling proud through personal goals.
- Social instinct: Feeling proud if the world recognizes their achievements.
- Sexual instinct: Feeling proud if they manage for others to be successful.

Depending on the environment or family they were born in, they will develop one need more that the other.

How is the ego structure upheld?

It upholds itself through the following mechanisms:

- Scotoma: Towards their own failures and desires.
- Selective attention: Towards their goals, achievements and triumphs.
- Defense mechanism: Identification.

Identification[52] is used by *Threes* to unconsciously incorporate attributes and characteristics of another person or role into their own personality and sense of self. Identification is a way of bolstering one's self-esteem by forming an imaginary or real alliance with an admired person or role, then taking on those characteristics.

When *Threes* model their own behavior after someone else or the idea they have of someone, they are usually not aware of doing so. For this reason, it becomes complicated for them to untangle who they really are from this image. In particular, *Threes* identify most with images of individuals who are admired in the *Three's* desired social context, and the image the *Three* identifies with often changes with the

---

[52] Lapid-Bogda, G. (2019), Enneagram Learning portal. www.theenneagramin-business.com

context. *Threes* also identify with what they *do* as a way to generate the admiration they want from others.

How do *Threes* think?

Basic fear
Of not being valuable, of having no personal worth.

Cognitive error
By thinking they are worthless, *Threes* begin to look for achievements and triumphs that make them look acceptable to others. As they disintegrate, they look more for external applause and less for self-recognition.

Motivation
To feel valuable.

Strategic skill of *Threes*

The ability they develop, according to Elaine De Beauport's[53] theory, is **motivational intelligence**, or the ability to move to get what you want, and to keep doing it throughout your life.

> *Motivational Intelligence implies the skill to know what I want, what arouses me, what excites me and moves me towards something. Therefore, a conscious examination of ourselves is needed, to find what it is we want, what expands us, shakes us, moves us: it is the knowledge of what excites us what allows us to keep the flame of life lit. Desire is the fuel of motivation. Only this fuel can keep you motivated and truly in love with life...When we stop wanting, we die. (pp. 210-215)*

---

[53] Beauport, E. y Díaz, A. (2008), *Las tres caras de la mente. El desarrollo de las inteligencias mentales, emocionales y del comportamiento (The Three Faces of Mind: Developing Your Mental, Emotional, and Behavioral Intelligences)*, 1ª ed., Caracas, Venezuela: Alfa Grupo Editorial.

Motivation is an intelligence that makes us achieve what we set our sights on. *Threes'* problem resides in their motivation being external rather than internal.

How to change the cognitive pattern of *Threes*

Motivation is the strength that materializes our achievements. It is not bad having motivation in life; what is bad, is having the wrong motivation. *Threes* seek to achieve goals that will lead them to obtain recognition from other people to feel valuable. The adjustment they must make is on the search and satisfaction of their own desires, not on the chase for goals that will make them look good to others.

Tips to improve if you are a *Three*

- Practice honesty, observe your tendency to disguise reality.
- See how your need to excel generates animosity in others.
- Learn to differentiate between who you really are and what you do.
- Stop focusing on your own interests and pay attention to the objectives of the group, your team or your family.
- Spend time for your family and social life; not everything is work.
- Value people for what they are and don't just use them to achieve your goals.
- The more honest you are about your failures, the closer you will experience others.

Four: The Creator

Authentic, romantic, original, intense

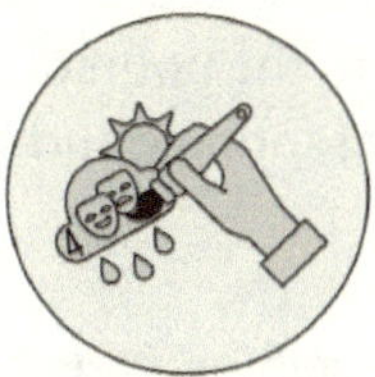

They want everything they do to be original. They are very good at expressing what other people cannot. They seek the intensity of life and to be different from others. They dream and fantasize about romantic moments. Their feelings are deeper than anyone else's. They either suffer a lot or enjoy a lot, and they may have sudden mood changes. They always have the feeling that there is something missing.

Characteristic behaviors

Automatic mode

They appreciate and create beauty. They are highly creative, intuitive and sincere. They look for originality in everything they do and many times they get carried away by their mood changes, emotions and impulses. They are introspective, passionate, sensitive and perceptive. They have a great facility to express what many cannot.

They like the intensity of life, and being different from others. They spend a lot of time and energy on conversations with themselves. They dream of and fantasize about romantic moments. They reach a depth of feelings greater than anyone else's. They suffer a lot or rejoice a lot, which can hinder their daily life. They have sudden mood swings, get carried away by their feelings and their current mood. Many times, they feel self-pity and pamper themselves, to the extent of justifying not fulfilling their responsibilities. They have a constant feeling of missing something.

Survival mode

In more threatening circumstances, they become manipulative, conceited, and they draw attention to themselves by playing the "victim". They hate, despise and are ashamed of themselves. They become depressive. They can even get to the point of self-destruction, using alcohol, food or drugs...or, they sabotage and blame themselves.

Rational mode

They act from their true self or essence. They know their mood swings, emotions and impulses very well, and they do not let themselves get carried away by them. They are introspective, passionate, sensitive and perceptive. They easily express what most people cannot. Therefore, they will be able to see both their qualities and needs in a balanced manner. "I see myself as a unique and incomparable person." The world is a place where everything comes from a single Origin, and Fours are connected to It. As a result of living connected to their essence, Fours know they are valuable, and that they are not lacking anything to be happy and complete.

How ego is formed

When the environment is not ideal for the *Four* child, it ceases to be nurturing and begins to be a threat. *"I need an emotional connection with my mother, and by not achieving it, I begin to feel lonely and abandoned."* Babies around eight months of age discover that their mother and they are not the same person, this phase is known as individuation. The baby lives the loss of something he considered as part of himself. The mother has the food and the child the hunger; The mother has warmth and the child is cold. This fact makes them feel needy because the mother has the satisfiers that he lacks.

As it is a reality that the *Four* child cannot meet their needs by themselves, an image of lack will be generated that they will drag throughout their lives, and will be sustained by a characteristic brain structure.

Core construct: "The world has what I lack"

Oscar Ichazo presented the concept of Holy Ideas, and *Fours'* would be Holy Origin[54]. *Fours'* healthy view is the ability to see that we all are unique and incomparable, and that we possess qualities no one else does.

In essence, *Fours* know themselves to be unique, and they do not feel any lack. This brings about the virtue of equanimity. They lack nothing and they do not need to reconnect to anything to regain their worth, because they know they have not lost it.

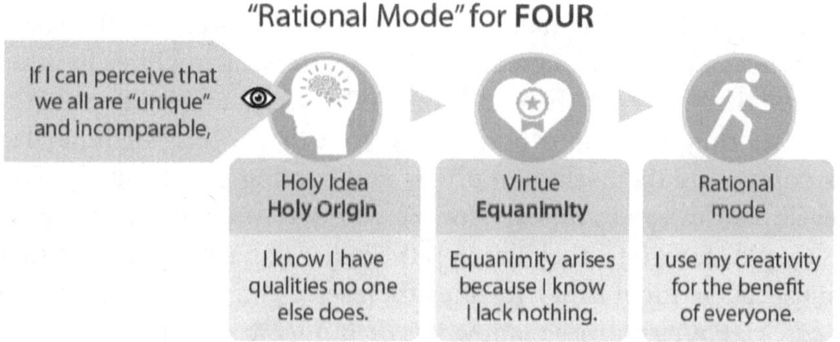

When *Fours* separate from their true self, due to the typical fear of their Enneatype, their view becomes distorted, and they begin to look for how to satisfy their need to connect with their personal value, instead of shifting their point of view or their reference point, realizing they never became separated. They choose to produce their feeling of being unique by looking for differences with others; this pattern will make them feel more and more disconnected from themselves and from the universe. This breaking point with their true self is what is described in some traditions as "loss of paradise". The more they focus on being different, the more they will disintegrate and distort their reality. Let us remember that the brain needs to solve issues to avoid stress, and it does not seek the truth, rather survival. *Fours* develop selective attention towards their lacks. *"Others have the happiness I lack."*

---

[54] In the business world, these terms are not well received, that is why I call them "healthy view of the world".

Naturally, they begin to fixate on satisfying their needs by playing the victim, so the world provides what they do not have.

Mental fixation: "I have to seek what I lack in order to satisfy it, by means of comparing myself to the world"

This fixation of paying attention selectively to what they lack, by means of comparison, generates the passion of *Fours*, which is envy. I like to define it as the belief that others have the happiness they lack. It is important to underline the fact that *Fours* do not usually covet material goods, and, actually, they have to work hard to see themselves as envious. *Fours* have a great talent for perceiving qualities in others, and see themselves as their admirers. What they cannot see is that the qualities they value in others stems from that feeling of inner lack. By comparing themselves to others and coming off as lacking, *Fours* develop a strategy to manage for the world to provide what they lack. As they disintegrate, they develop the belief of having the right to get things. Their inner child justifies themselves: *"Since I have so many needs, and others have so much, it is their duty to satisfy them."*

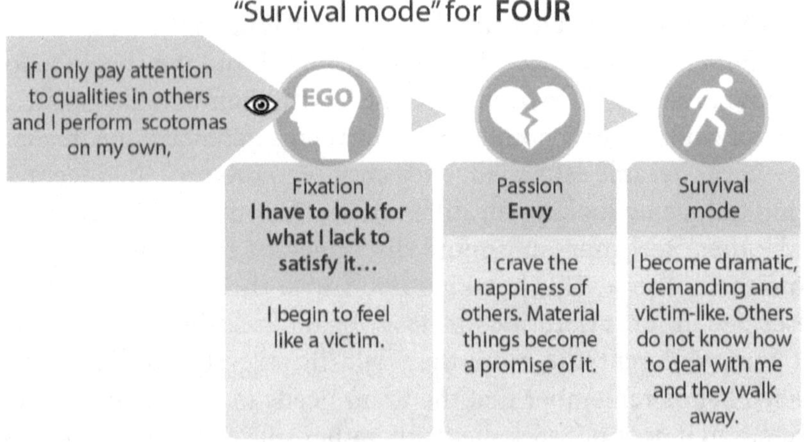

This strategy will manifest, as in all Enneatypes, through one of the three instincts, which in the case of *Fours* are:

- Preservation instinct: Suffer in solitude to earn love.
- Social instinct: Earn love and attention by showing suffering openly.
- Sexual instinct: Make others suffer as vindication for not having had the same chances.

How is the ego structure upheld?

It upholds itself through the following mechanisms:

- Scotoma: Towards their qualities and abilities.
- Selective attention: Towards their needs and lacks.
- Defense mechanism: Introjection.

Introjection[55] is a counterintuitive defense mechanism. Instead of repelling critical information and negative experiences that can cause them anxiety or pain, *Fours* introject the information – that is, they fully absorb, internalize, and incorporate this perceived information into their sense of self without discerning whether or not it is true or useful. *Fours* introject negative information – and repel positive data – about themselves as a way of coping with painful information and neutralizing external threats. They prefer to deal with self-inflicted damage rather than having to respond to criticism or rejection from others.

The defense mechanism is triggered most strongly when they feel anxious about impending negative feedback or when they become close to others and then worry about being rejected. Lacking clear boundaries to differentiate what to internalize and what to not take seriously, combined with their tendency to absorb negative data but reject positive information, *Fours* continuously defend against not feeling good enough. Ironically, *Fours* do not realize that the very defense mechanism they use to fend off negative information actually creates their reservoir of negative self-perception.

---

[55] Lapid-Bogda, G. (2019), Enneagram Learning portal. www.theenneagramin-business.com

How do *Fours* think?

Basic fear
Of lacking identity or personal meaning.

Cognitive error
To think they lack what they see in others, which generates a feeling of scarcity that makes them feel and act like a victim in life to draw others' attention. They over-identify with their emotional states and mood swings, especially negative ones. Since their moods change constantly, their identity does the same. This brings about great emotional instability.

Motivation
Managing to find what makes them feel unique.

Strategic skill of *Fours*

The ability *Fours* develop, according to Elaine De Beauport's[56] theory, is **mood intelligence**, which enables them to enter an emotion, letting themselves be affected by it, and exiting it once they have obtained the information they desired.

> *Mood intelligence allows us to fluctuate, to move and to develop mastery in going in and out of emotions, experiencing the information each emotion brings, exiting them when appropriate.*
>
> *The same way ideas and images produced by the neocortex possess information for us, emotions contain information. Emotions are information transmitted from within. In daily life, the lack of emotional information may make you inefficient, and its repression may cause damage or illness...Emotions provide a different personal text than mental reactions. (pp. 172-173)*

[56] Beauport, E. y Díaz, A. (2008), *Las tres caras de la mente. El desarrollo de las inteligencias mentales, emocionales y del comportamiento (The Three Faces of Mind: Developing Your Mental, Emotional, and Behavioral Intelligences)*, 1ª ed., Caracas, Venezuela: Alfa Grupo Editorial.

Another function of this intelligence is to access the brain's natural chemicals, such as endorphins, serotonin, dopamine, etc. These drugs regulate the stillness-agitation state of the organism. In turn, we know it is important to be able to access the complete range of emotions, to ensure the proper development of the organism: from the sadness that calms, to the rage that stimulates. Fours sense this intelligence will provide the information they need about themselves; by not having a determined identity, and become stuck in these emotional changes, looking for information that allows them to find their much-longed-for identity.

How to change the cognitive pattern of *Fours*

Four has to be taught they are already unique, and that they have to do nothing more to be different. They need to learn to pay attention to their true qualities, and to realize that what they think of as lacks, many times are not their own needs, but triggers of suffering provoked by their EGO. Doing the exercise of expressing gratitude for ten good things they have, every day, will be helpful to them.

Tips to improve if you are a *Four*

- Accept yourself, love yourself and value yourself.
- Value your qualities and stop envying others.
- Set a goal, order yourself and work on it; you will be surprised by your creativity.
- Remember that you are more than your feelings; don't over identify with them. Avoid being dominated and ruined by them.
- Stop dreaming, avoid self-pity, don't waste your time and get to work!
- Learn not to make decisions when you find yourself in a storm of emotions.
- Be grateful every day for all the good things you do have: a family, a good job…

Five: The Observer

Independent, analytical, withdrawn, inquisitive

Fives focus deeply on what they like and may neglect other things. They tend to live in their heads and seek to understand the world around them. They have a hard time with physical work and are not very good at expressing their emotions. They keep an emotional distance from others and may come across as cold or insensitive.

Characteristic behaviors

Automatic mode

They are objective, analytical and observant. They are passionate about knowledge, thought and silence. They perceive life from a whole, and, at the same time, they delve into it to the smallest detail. They like to discover, to disassemble, to investigate the origin of things, and to find out why they are like they are. They focus deeply on what they like, and they neglect the rest. They keep an emotional distance with others. They tend to be isolated, independent and austere. They live in their mind, where they can get lost. They do not like socializing much. They have trouble expressing their emotions and they are clumsy with physical contact. They are very skilled at isolating themselves from people, situations and their own feelings.

Survival mode

In more threatening circumstances, they become negative, greedy, miserly, and intellectually arrogant; they isolate themselves completely from the world and from emotion. They obsess with strange ideas, and they become mentally unstable.

Rational mode

They are capable of participating with their environment in a committed manner, and in real time. They are connected to their emotions and they use their great intellectual ability to improve the world. They are the pioneers, innovators, and inventors of our world. *"The world is a safe place, where my needs are well received and tended to in the moment they arise, even intellectual ones. It is not necessary to hoard information, since it will be available when needed."*

How ego is formed

The *Five* child feels that their needs are not satisfied at all and their way of solving it is by minimizing them. *"I am disconnected from my physical and emotional needs."* As they disintegrate, they seek for more distance to be able to observe and understand the world and its surroundings. The further they move away, the greater their disconnection and the less ability to see their needs.

Fives perceive that the environment does not meet their needs, but demand a lot from themselves. Therefore, they seek to move away emotionally and physically, and their attention will be focused on putting distance between the environment and themselves and acquiring skills that allow them to understand it in order to survive. Their vision or construction of the world will be a consequence of this way of seeing it.

Core construct: The world is invasive; it demands too much and I do not understand it

Fives' Holy Idea, according to Ichazo, is omniscience[57], which can be explained as the ability to know what is needed at the right time, and that is to me the healthy view of *Fives*. An example of this wisdom is the one some elders or natives naturally have. They understand the

---

[57] In the business world, these terms are not well received, that is why I call them "healthy view of the world".

world and its functioning without ever having studied. When a person lives with that conviction, that they know what they need to know, they have no feeling of lack or attachment to either material things or knowledge. The ability to see that aspect of reality without distortion or judgment is what I call healthy view, and, to my understanding, it is the equivalent to Ichazo's Holy Ideas.

When *Fives* have tasted true knowledge, they live without attachment. In essence, *Fives* possess "Wisdom" of the world naturally, and, therefore, the virtue of nonattachment arises in them.

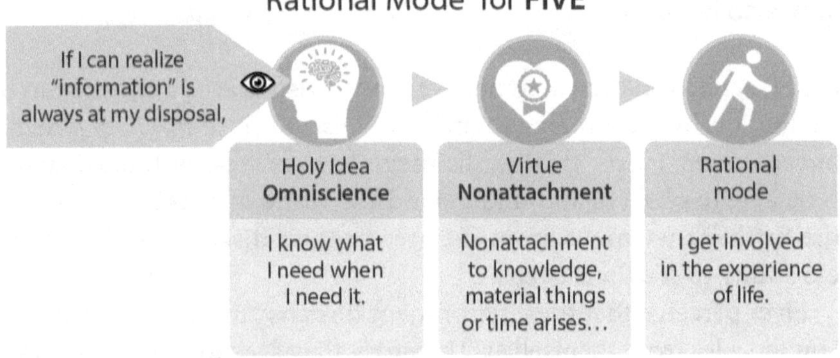

Mental fixation of Fives: "I need to accumulate knowledge to understand"

This need to possess information to have security generates their passion, which is greed. It is the need to hoard knowledge and information for fear of lacking them when required – it is not material things that they yearn for, it is knowledge and understanding. In order to learn and accumulate knowledge; space, distance and solitude are required. So, *Fives* separate from their essence, tend to isolate themselves more to be able to study and understand, which makes them feel less skilled at dealing with interpersonal relations. The child thinks: "*I do not understand the world or these adults; I have to prepare myself more.*"

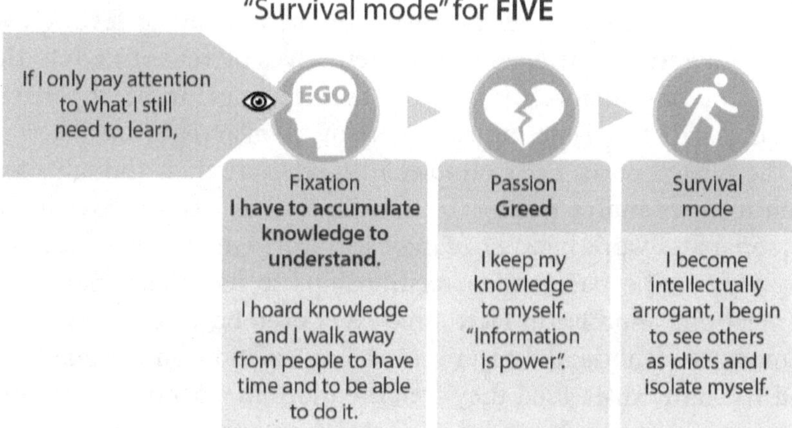

This strategy will manifest, as in all Enneatypes, through one of the three instincts, which in the case of *Fives* are:

- Preservation instinct: By keeping themselves isolated in their sanctuary.
- Social instinct: By hoarding information and knowledge.
- Sexual instinct: By looking for someone worthy of sharing their knowledge with.

How is the ego structure upheld?

Ego's mechanisms of *Fives* are the following:

- Scotoma: Towards physical and emotional needs.
- Selective attention: Towards the knowledge they still need to acquire.
- Defense mechanism: Isolation.

Isolation[58] occurs in *Fives* as a way for them to avoid feeling over-whelmed and empty. *Fives* isolate themselves by retreating into their minds, cutting themselves off from their feelings, and compartmen-talizing – that is, isolating each part of themselves from the whole or the related parts. For example, *Fives* separate their thoughts from their feelings and/or feelings from behaviors, as well as separate their personal and work lives. *Fives* may also isolate themselves from other people and separate their relationships so that their friends never meet one another; in fact, some *Fives* even have secret lives. *Fives* demonstrate subtle and blatant forms of isolation on a regular basis and the more distressed they feel, the more this occurs. In addition, *Fives* who have done a great deal of self-development work still utilize this defense mechanism, but they do so with more subtlety.

How do *Fives* think?

Basic fear
Of not being capable or intelligent.

Cognitive error
To think that to understand the world around them, they need to be separated from it. The more stressed they are, the more they separate from the world, and the less they understand it. They tend to replace experience with concepts of it. It would be like knowing by heart the technique of swimming, but without ever getting into the water. They put everything into systems and they classify people and situations as if they were knowledge.

Motivation
To understand the world around them in order to feel capable.

---

[58] Lapid-Bogda, G. (2019), Enneagram Learning portal. www.theenneagramin-business.com

Strategic skill of *Fives*

The ability they develop, according to Elaine De Beauport's[59] theory, is **rational intelligence**, which is responsible for logical and analytical sequential thought, as well as for cause-and-effect thought.

> *Rational intelligence has been widely accepted not only as the basis of Western civilization, but also as a synonym for the word intelligence. In recent years, great unrest has come up due to the lack of precise thought in our culture, and to a potential decadence of rational intelligence. Often, we fail when we base our thought in selected reasoning. I think this decline of reason may be explained by our desire to be socially accepted, to be polite and well-mannered, which we can usually accomplish by using slightly ambiguous phrases, mixing images and feelings along with thoughts and avoiding the accuracy required by rational thought. (p. 45)*

The problem resides not in the ability to be rational but rather in the fact that *Fives* do it by separating themselves from situations and people to have greater observation skills, which allow them, in turn, to be more objective. This causes them to feel increasingly isolated from others and to be perceived as cold and uninterested.

How to change the cognitive pattern of *Fives*

When *Fives* have low social intelligence, it is hard work for them to interact with others. Their constant fear of not knowing what to do or what to say, makes them feel rejected by and distanced from others. They are highly observant and analytical, and that is why it will be useful for them to notice that others do not really know what to do as

---

[59] Beauport, E. y Díaz, A. (2008), *Las tres caras de la mente. El desarrollo de las inteligencias mentales, emocionales y del comportamiento (The Three Faces of Mind: Developing Your Mental, Emotional, and Behavioral Intelligences)*, 1ª ed., Caracas, Venezuela: Alfa Grupo Editorial.

well, and that they also make mistakes. This will allow them to intervene and start interacting more easily.

If *Fives* have poor physical skills, they can join the football team, for example, by keeping statistics and by being the coach's assistant, so their observation qualities are recognized by the group and they feel more integrated. Team games are difficult for them; they would rather do something on their own, such as martial arts or indoor climbing, which allow them to socialize in a limited manner, but depending entirely on their personal abilities. Search for some activity that allows the mental abilities of *Fives* to be applied in their physical activities.

Tips to improve if you are a *Five*

- Balance observation with participation.
- Dare to express your opinion.
- Don't think so much about what you are going to say while others are speaking.
- Do not disappear unexpectedly without giving explanations.
- Strive to be more generous with your time, your information and your energy.
- When you disagree with something, instead of withdrawing in silence or calling them "fools", look for another way to express your ideas.
- Learn to differentiate between information and knowledge. It is one thing to accumulate data and another to experience it in your body and in your heart and make it part of you.

Six: The Questioner

Responsible, reliable, committed, ambivalent

Certainty is most important to them. They like things to be clear and to know where they stand. They hesitate a lot before making a decision. They are always on the lookout for danger, for what may go wrong as well as for the intentions of others so they are not taken by surprise. They are skeptical and questioning, with inquisitive and watchful minds. When they feel anxious, their mind wanders to the worst possible scenario. They are either very loyal to authority or they rebel completely against it.

Characteristic behaviors

Automatic mode

They are responsible, hard-working, committed and loyal. They are cooperative and able to work in teams. They are likeable and caring: they enjoy getting and joining friends together, as well as family. Their safety and of those close to them are very important. They have an inquisitive and vigilant mind. They are skeptical and challenging. They like to keep things clear, and to know where they are standing. They hesitate a lot before making a decision. They are cautious and prudent. They are always alert of danger, of what can go wrong, of others' hidden intentions, so they do not take them by surprise. When they feel preoccupied and anxious, their mind drifts to the worst possible scenario. They are either very loyal to authority, or they rebel completely against it.

Survival mode

In more threatening circumstances, they become extremely vigilant, insecure, nervous and cowardly; paranoid as well. They can overreact to everything, becoming negative, defensive and aggressive.

Rational mode

The quality of six is being connected to their environment, they have plenty of self-confidence; they are brave, assertive and decisive. *"I perceive reality without distortion and I trust life to feel supported"*. They have what is known as operational intelligence, that is, decision-making intelligence. They draw their energy from being present in reality, which gives them the assurance that everything will be alright. They do what they have to do without expecting recognition, and they respond to life with certainty and confidence.

How ego is formed

When *Sixes* disconnect from their essence, they lose their operational intelligence and seek to replace it with outside help. *"I have the feeling of having lost my orientation, I am very anxious."*

Sixes develop attachment to the protective figure that is traditionally represented by the father; they learn from these father figures how to protect and guide themselves, as well as how to become independent from the mother. When this father figure does not provide the security *Sixes* need to accomplish this, or provides it in excess, they feel unprotected or distrust their ability to fend for themselves, so throughout their life, they look for figures that provide them with the security that they consider incapable of giving themselves.

This attachment to the protective figure causes the *Six* child to form an image of himself as weak and unable to survive on his own. *Sixes* will draw the conclusion that they must be aware of the dangers to prevent them in time and to avoid catastrophes. *Sixes* will develop an excellent ability to detect signs of threat, incongruity or lies around them. Their attention will be focused on detecting the danger and their vision or construction of the world will be a consequence of this way of seeing it.

Core construct: The world is not a safe place. I must be on the lookout for danger signals in the environment, in people or in situations

Oscar Ichazo presented the concept of Holy Ideas, and *Six's* is Holy Faith[60]. The healthy view of the *Six* is the ability to know we are all supported by the universe, and that everything that happens is for a greater good.

In essence, *Sixes* have "faith" or trust in life. They respond to life with certainty and they are humble people, despite being great. By having this certainty, the virtue of the *Six* arises, which is courage before life.

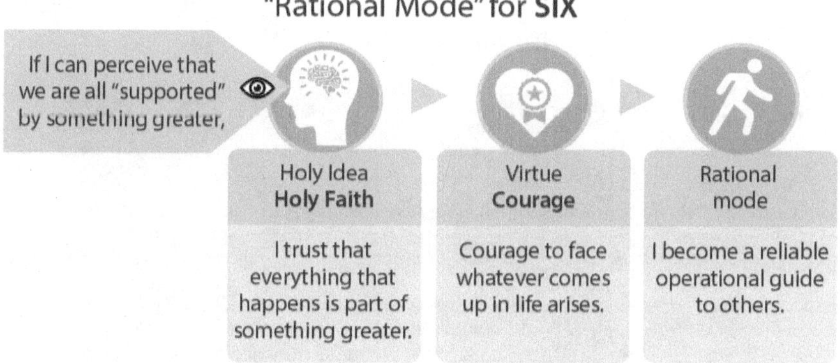

When *Sixes* separate from their essence, due to the typical fear of their Enneatype, their view becomes distorted, and they begin to look for the way to satisfy their need for safety. Instead of looking for it in what already is, they separate from their essence, from the UNIVERSE, from GOD; they choose to produce it instead of shifting their point of view or reference point. This breaking point with their BEING is what is described in some traditions as "loss of paradise". The more they focus on looking for safety, the more they will disintegrate, and reality will distort. The way in which their brain solves is known

---

[60] In the business world, these terms are not well received, that is why I call them "healthy view of the world".

in the Enneagram as mental fixation. *Sixes* start to fixate on looking for safety within their own means or in the world around them.

Mental fixation: "I have to look for my safety"

This fixation of looking for safety and detecting danger triggers fear, which either paralyzes them or propels them to fight. As *Sixes* disintegrate, they become increasingly afraid, which is the typical passion of this Enneatype. Their strategy towards life will be to detect danger in order to defeat it, or to avoid it by running away from it. The child thinks: *"My parents do not know how to take care of me, so I must do it myself."*

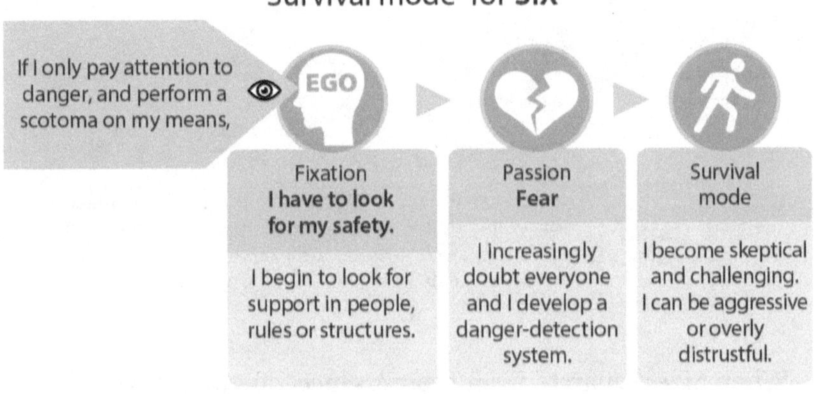

This strategy will manifest, as in all Enneatypes, through one of the three instincts, which in the case of *Sixes* are:

- Preservation instinct: They look for security by their own means.
- Social instinct: They look for safety by complying with rules and belonging to well-structured organizations.
- Sexual instinct: They look for safety by creating meaningful relationships that can provide it.

Depending on the environment or family they were born in, they will develop one need more that the other.

How is the ego structure upheld?

Ego's mechanisms

- Scotoma: Towards my skills and tools to face danger.
- Selective attention: Towards dangers that might come up.
- Defense mechanism: Projection

Projection[61] is a psychological defense mechanism in which individuals unconsciously attribute their own unacceptable, unwanted, or disowned thoughts, emotions, motivations, attributes, and/or behaviors to others. While the projection may be positive or negative, it occurs because the individuals who are projecting perceive the projected attributes as difficult to acknowledge or threatening to believe about themselves. Because *Sixes* make these attributions unconsciously, they imagine that they are true, although at a deeper level they are not entirely certain about this. Although *Sixes* use projection as a way to create some certainty and reduce their anxiety in ambiguous, uncertain, or potentially dangerous situations, these projections – particularly if they are negative in nature – ironically raise the *Six's* anxiety level. In addition, when *Sixes* project either something negative or positive that is untrue, they create a false reality without knowing they are doing so. Although *Sixes* project on an ongoing basis, they project most often and most intensely when they are anxious. The more anxiety they feel, the more difficult it becomes for *Sixes* to differentiate between a projection and an insight – that is, something that is true. *Sixes* also project positive information and feelings, including idealizing those who they regard highly.

---

[61] Lapid-Bogda, G. (2019), Enneagram Learning portal. www.theenneagraminbusiness.com

How do *Sixes* think?

Basic fear
Of being incapable of fending for themselves.

Cognitive error
They see the world as dangerous, and they consider themselves incapable of facing such dangers, which is why they look for safety in people, rules and structures. They believe the guidance and support they need come from structures, people or social relations, because they find themselves in constant need of evaluating the reliability of such safety factors. They do this instead of seeking their instinct or internal guide, which will never betray them.

Motivation
Achieve autonomy and security.

Strategic skill of *Sixes*

The skill they develop, according to Elaine De Beauport's[62] theory, is **associative intelligence**, which refers to the skill of connecting data and creating links with what they want to associate with. The *Sixes'* difficulty would be in not being able to reach a decision or conclusion on what is the best option, since they tend to over-analyze things.

> *For its part, association is characteristic to the right hemisphere. Associating is the ability to make fortuitous rather than sequential connections: free flights, leaps, relations made out of pleasure or inclination, of preferences, forms and nuances. Association is relating to the purpose of being open to new connections; or to discover casually, stopping along the road, jumping obstacles, go-*

---

[62] Beauport, E. y Díaz, A. (2008), *Las tres caras de la mente. El desarrollo de las inteligencias mentales, emocionales y del comportamiento (The Three Faces of Mind: Developing Your Mental, Emotional, and Behavioral Intelligences)*, 1ª ed., Caracas, Venezuela: Alfa Grupo Editorial.

ing around or further than anything seeming to be a fixed proce-dure...However, we might as well ask ourselves whether this cre-ative process is exclusive to artists, or if it needs to be available for every thinking being. (p. 42)

Associative intelligence is neither the opposite of rational in-telligence nor the replacement of rational thought. They are twin thought processes. Rational intelligence makes connections se-quentially, and associative intelligence makes them disregarding sequence. On certain cases, reasoning is appropriate, and in other cases, associating is. Both intelligences are essential to the think-ing mind. A person may need to be extremely rational when fol-lowing instructions on the computer, when handling money or personal affairs that require precision and conclusion. The same person may need to be extremely associative when meeting some-one for the first time, and this requires finding something, upon first look, they like; then, to express it, and thus begin to relate. When we use associative thought, we establish connections with people, places, ideas, objects, colors and concepts, among other things. (p. 57)

As it has been noticed in the Enneagram, the danger people who favor this type of intelligence are in, is being unable to reach conclusions, and becoming trapped in the realm of possibilities. *Sixes* have a hard time making decisions and sticking to them, since their brain is used to seeing and analyzing every existing possibility, even in the simplest of things, like buying a pair of shoes.

The problem does not reside in using that intelligence; but in fa-voring it, since we are limiting our human potential and our possibil-ities to understand the environment.

The *Six's* ego restricts the brain to only perform this type of anal-ysis, and it limits their decision-making ability. That is why they are constantly going through data, looking for information that can be used to detect potential danger. As it always happens, the overuse of a positive ability becomes a flaw, which in this case would be the lack of objectivity, leading to paralysis. The counterphobic *Six* makes rash decisions to counteract this trait.

How to change the cognitive pattern of *Sixes*

Taking advantage of what we already know, we realize that it is convenient for this Enneatype to develop rational intelligence. That is, teaching them to look at the data they have under an objective and rational perspective. The same thing happens with their fears: they will have to learn to shred them apart and look at them objectively.

Another beneficial thing for *Sixes* is to notice how often their catastrophic thoughts come true; in this way, they will be able to reframe their fears within objective reality.

Making *Sixes* move can be very useful, since it takes them out of the thinking center and connects them to their body and to the present.

Integrated *Sixes* trust that they are sustained and safe, but when they are stressed or feel threatened, they disintegrate and the ego begins to seek to generate security by detecting the dangerous ones that lurk and be alert to them.

Tips to improve if you are a *Six*

- Look for reasons to trust, instead of looking for reasons to distrust.
- Trust more in yourself and your own abilities.
- Even if you doubt and feel fear, dare to try.
- Use your skills as a "devil's advocate" but with the intention
- of helping, instead of "pricking the balloon" compulsively.
- Be careful with your internal dialogue, "How dangerous, no
- I can't, it's very difficult! Your words are orders to your brain.
- Share and compare your fears with other people's fears.
- You will realize how your mind exaggerates and distorts reality.

Seven: The Animator

Hyperactive, dreamy, flexible, fun

They always look for the opportunities and resources of life. They like freedom and believe that opportunities will not be there forever, so they have to grab them while they last. They constantly seek new and stimulating experiences and are innovative, although they might have a hard time finishing what they start. They may not be very committed, and they are easily distracted.

Characteristic behaviors

Automatic mode

They are extroverted, likeable and generous. They are perceptive, creative and they have great skill to synthesize and connect different ideas. They are charming and dreamy. They plan more than they can do. They look for pleasant and fun things and get bored and distracted easily, since they need new experiences and sensations that stimulate them. They tend to see the good and adventurous side of life to avoid pain and suffering. They enjoy freedom; they cannot stand being told what to do. They want to do everything and miss nothing. It is difficult for them to commit, because they prefer to have several options available.

Survival mode

In more threatening circumstances they become selfish, abusive and opportunistic and may exhibit impulsive, aggressive and childish behaviors. There is no limit to anything! They also have addictive and self-destructive tendencies: alcohol, drugs, and generalized excess.

Rational mode

Sevens know what rejoicing in living life to the fullest means and know how to be in the present moment. They commit, concentrate and finish what they start without diverting their attention to pleasure. They are grateful and experience life deeply. They let themselves be captivated by the wonders of life. They contact their true self, and have a profound feeling of what limitless kindness is. "I enjoy every moment of life, and I have the ability to see the light, even in the worst moments." They have real idealism, and know that happiness is a process in which helping other people is always involved.

How ego is formed

When *Sevens* separate from their essence, they begin to experience fear and anxiety as all the mental types. The way in which their ego solves this problem is by planning strategies that may provide them with resources while they last. The problem is that this strategy may become addictive, and it makes *Sevens* miss out on the experience of reality. This mental pattern is what produces gluttony, the passion of this Enneatype.

An example would be that the *Seven* child is in his crib at midnight, and he cannot perceive the mother's presence. To mammals, this means abandonment, and biologically it means the risk of being attacked by a predator. *Sevens* learn to escape the present and to fantasize a better future, based on past experiences. That is, the child thinks: *"My mother is not available, but when the sun comes up, she will appear with a big bottle of warm milk, and she will hold me in her arms"*.

Sevens learned to cut off the dark side of life when they felt their needs were not satisfied properly. They learned to imagine themselves in that pleasant future to avoid the fear of feeling helpless and abandoned. This becomes their habitual way to face life, until they forget to let themselves be affected by the present. They develop the belief that if they come in contact with pain, they will become trapped there. The result is a pathologically enthusiastic person.

Core construct: The world is a fun place, and we must have a good time

Oscar Ichazo presented the concept of Holy Ideas, and *Sevens'* is the thought that everything is ruled by a Holy Plan[63]. The healthy view of *Sevens* is the ability to see that everything that happens is part of a greater plan, and that everything has meaning. *Sevens'* task is not making plans but rather enjoying the daily gift of life and the plan that was already perfectly created for them by the Universe. Their ability to enjoy what life offers them is a great gift for everyone around them. That is true optimism: to be able to see the positive side of everything that happens in life, instead of avoiding the negative parts and making plans that keep them stimulated. I like to remind *Sevens* that no one needs a lamp when the sun is shining, and that their light was made to illuminate when the path of others is dark. Looking at situations with realistic optimism is what I call healthy view, and, to my understanding, it is the equivalent to Ichazo's Holy Ideas.

In essence, *Sevens* are able to perceive the "plan" life designs, and then the virtue of Temperance arises in them, since they stop trying to create enjoyment and focus on enjoying what is the result of a greater plan.

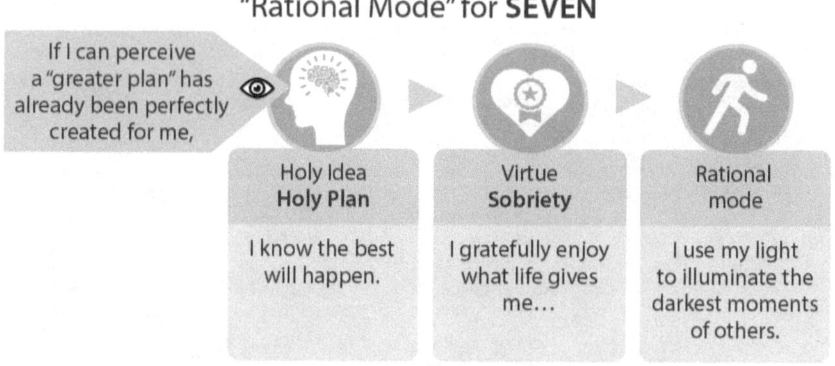

---

[63] In the business world, these terms are not well received, that is why I call them "healthy view of the world".

When *Sevens* separate from their essence due to the typical fear of their Enneatype, their view becomes distorted, and they begin to look for how to satisfy their need to find joy. Instead of seeking to enjoy what happens to them, they separate from their essence, from the UNIVERSE, from GOD; they choose to produce it instead of shifting their point of view or reference point. The more they focus on planning fun things for the future, the more they will disintegrate and their reality will distort. The way in which they solve this issue is known in the Enneagram as mental fixation, and *Sevens* begin to fixate on wanting to plan pleasant or positive situations that keep them stimulated.

Mental fixation: "I have to plan for tomorrow to avoid suffering"

This fixation of seeking stimulation through anticipation keeps them from enjoying the present. Despite looking like they enjoy life and sharing that feeling with others, they are not enjoying themselves. That is why the passion of gluttony arises, since it takes longer to get to the longed-for moment than to be disappointed by it, and realizing that the much-longed-for joy was not there either. So, their search for enjoyment starts all over again and they start planning next activity without even finishing the present one.

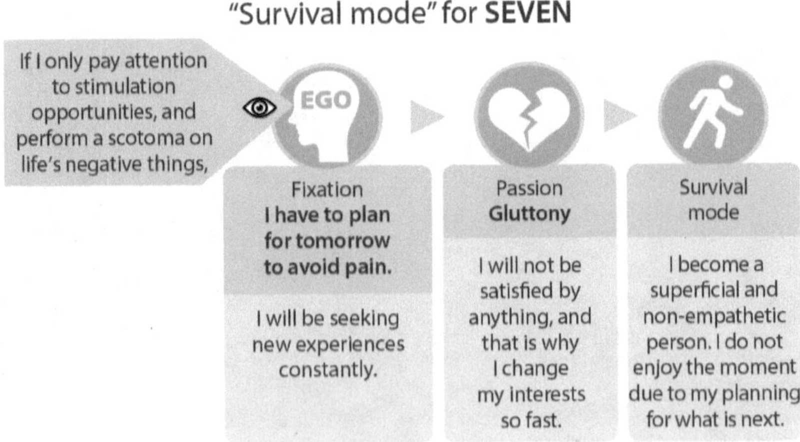

This strategy will manifest, as in all Enneatypes, through one of the three instincts, which in the case of *Sevens* are:

- Preservation instinct: I seek to avoid pain by creating a friendship network.
- Social instinct: I seek to avoid pain by sacrificing myself and being helpful.
- Sexual instinct: I seek to avoid pain by enjoying the good things life gives me.

How is the ego structure upheld?

Mechanisms of the ego:

- Scotoma: Towards opportunities, and positive and fun things.
- Selective attention: Towards pain and negative things.
- Defense mechanism: Rationalization

Rationalization[64] is used by *Sevens* to explain unacceptable thoughts, feelings, and behaviors in a way that entirely avoids or obscures their true motivations, intentions, or the effects of the behavior. When *Sevens* rationalize, they do so by positive reframing – that is, justifying their behavior by explaining it in highly positive terms. *Sevens* use reframing to avoid pain, discomfort, sadness, guilt, and anxiety, as well as to avoid taking personal responsibility for what has occurred.

Sevens rationalize by reframing primarily when they feel or anticipate feeling distressed. They also reframe ideas as part of the way they think; this can be an asset when they generate new ways of doing things or engage in creative problem solving. In these positive instances, *Sevens* may take an issue such as an impending reorganization about which people are anxious and say, "Yes, but the reorganization also provides us with the opportunity to reexamine how we do things and to create enormous improvements." However, when *Sevens* ratio-

---

[64] Lapid-Bogda, G. (2019), Enneagram Learning portal. www.theenneagramin-business.com

nalize their own unacceptable behavior, it becomes a problem both for them and those around them.

How do *Sevens* think?

Basic fear
Of becoming trapped in pain or scarcity.

Cognitive error
Sevens think that they have to take opportunities while they last and avoid pain at all costs. This need to avoid triggers a constant need for stimulation, which will make them feel emptier and more anxious than if they face pain when it comes up. They think they will achieve satisfaction and happiness by planning and anticipating the future, instead of learning how to live and enjoy the present. They live anticipating experiences, and, therefore, they do not enjoy them at all.

Motivation
To enjoy life to the fullest.

Strategic skill of *Sevens*

The ability *Sevens* develop, according to Elaine De Beauport's[65] theory, is **spatial, visual and auditory intelligence**, which is another intelligence we find in the right hemisphere of the neocortex. It enables us to perceive image and sound, but especially to foresee situations. It also helps us plan and imagine consequences.

Image configuration, imagination, fantasy and hypothesis are all mental functions of the spatial-visual intelligence, which you can

---

[65] Beauport, E. y Díaz, A. (2008), *Las tres caras de la mente. El desarrollo de las inteligencias mentales, emocionales y del comportamiento (The Three Faces of Mind: Developing Your Mental, Emotional, and Behavioral Intelligences)*, 1ª ed., Caracas, Venezuela: Alfa Grupo Editorial.

honor, make true and make part of your mental skill. By form-ing images in your mind, you are able to not only enrich your life and improve your brain's power, but to use those images as a guide to your daily life as well. Images are information, real infor-mation, usable in whichever layer of reality you wish to inhabit: imaginary, subtle or externally real. Visual-spatial intelligence is a mental process that activates the neocortex on a more profound level than associative intelligence. Use it to access more informa-tion about yourself. (p. 81)

People with this Enneatype have great skill to connect ideas; what they often lack is the discipline to follow a more rational mental order. Contrasting this intelligence to reality will trigger a feeling of order and safety. *Sevens* will foresee pleasant situations as a mechanism to run away from a present they perceive as unpleasant or painful. Fur-thermore, if they do not apply their mental ability to the present, they will miss out on what is happening right now, to become lost in the infinite realm of possibilities and fantasy. People whose visual-spatial intelligence is highly developed tend to come off as dreamy and play-ful, despite adding to the environment their ability to be innovative and flexible.

How to change the cognitive pattern of *Sevens*

Metaphorically, we can say *Sevens* seek to feel the experience of living in a toy store, thinking of all the toys they can buy, but they forget that the only way to really enjoy the toy is to choose it and buy it. If deci-sions are not made, there is nothing there... and one lives in perma-nent dissatisfaction. Therefore, they have to learn to make decisions and to live with their consequences.

Another aspect to work with is to make *Sevens* see that light and optimism are helpful when people are sad. When *Sevens* bring their light and joy to people who need them, their life takes on deep mean-ing, and they find the true joy they had been looking so hard for.

Tips to improve if you are a *Seven*

- Do not promise what you cannot accomplish.
- Slow down and choose priorities. *"He who focuses upon everything has, in fact, no focus."*
- Have discipline, focus on one thing and commit to finishing it. Ask yourself what the negative part of the situation is and face it.
- Look at the tendency you have to justify your mistakes and fails
- without assuming responsibility.
- Learn to listen and empathize, instead of thinking ahead of an ingenious response that breaks the ice.

Eight: The Wrestler

Natural leader, direct, decided, assertive

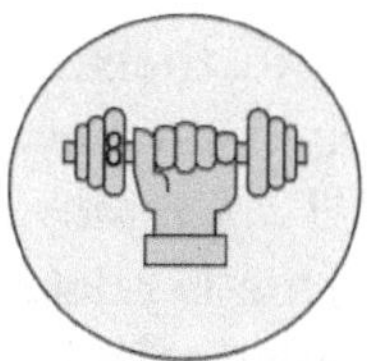

Generous and protective, they are energetic and enthusiastic towards life and work. They inspire others to follow and trust them. They think big. They like control and power. They enjoy confrontation and difficult challenges where they can test themselves. They hate weakness and suffering, which is why they repress anyone who shows these things. Their word is the law, which is why they easily break the rules.

Characteristic behaviors

Automatic mode

They are natural leaders. They are direct, determined and assertive. They are generous and protective. They are energetic and enthusiastic towards life and towards work. They inspire others to follow and trust them. They think big! They are dominant, they like control and power and to make things happen. They put down any manifestation of weakness or suffering so they hate others to remind them of what they fear so much about themselves. They are competitive and like confrontation and difficult challenges to prove themselves. They easily detect falsehood and faked strength. Their word is law, so they easily break rules. They are impulsive and they let themselves get carried away by excess everywhere. They may confront, make big promises and intimidate people to get what they want.

Survival mode

In more threatening circumstances, they become extremely aggressive, overbearing, sadistic, deceitful and manipulative just to get their way. They become punishing, possessive and controlling with others. They can lose control and destroy everything around.

Rational mode

When *Eights* are connected to their essence, they use their power and energy constructively. They have the ability to perceive the world in an innocent way. *"I am totally and deeply human, with an amazing simplicity."* This virtue is related to children, and it allows *Eights* to live without manipulating, but as sincere, direct and loving.

How ego is formed

Eights feel they lost the protection they had the right to very early in life. They feel that they did not get what they need from the environment, and ceased to feel loved and protected. In response, their ego makes them protect themselves and others from a very young age. *"Life is a struggle. I live in constant strife."*

Similar to Fours, *Eights* feel that something has been lost. And their ego reacts to that loss instead of trying to understand its origin. *Eights* think that someone is responsible for their loss and seek revenge. In this fixation, they tend to see everything as a struggle, as something to overcome. They learn to fight to get what they need.

Since the *Eights* develop the belief that the world belongs to the strong, they avoid being in touch with their vulnerability at all costs. They will seek to produce an image of a strong and invulnerable person, which will characterize them throughout their life and that will be held by a specific brain structure.

Core construct: The world belongs to the strong

Oscar Ichazo presented the concept of Holy Ideas, and *Eight*'s would be Holy Truth[66]. The healthy view of *Eights* is the ability to see that there

---

[66] In the business world, these terms are not well received, that is why I call them

is only one Truth. Healthy view is the ability to see an aspect of reality without distortion or judgment, and, to my understanding, it is the equivalent to Ichazo's Holy Ideas.

In essence, the *Eights* seek the truth and do not deceive themselves. They always show themselves in an authentic way, and look at the world through their virtue, which is innocence. They expect everyone to do the same.

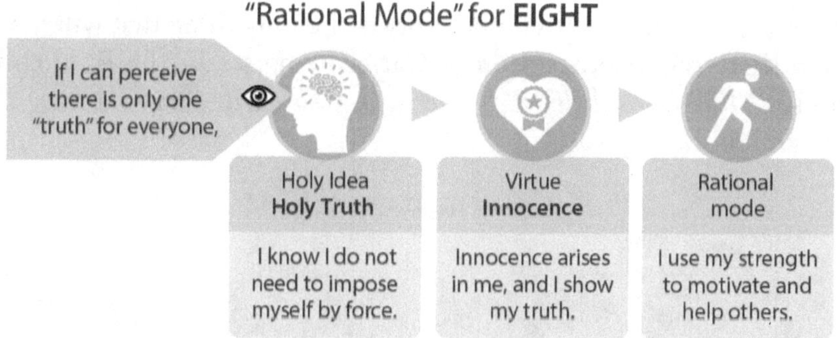

When *Eights* realize that not everyone shows their truth in the same way, they feel betrayed. They feel that their innocence was taken from them too soon. This feeling is common in many *Eights*, who say they had to grow up and mature very young. By separating from their essence due to the fear of being vulnerable, their view becomes distorted and they begin to look for a way to impose their Truth, instead of shifting their view or reference point in order to find it again. They choose to produce their own truth and to impose it on others by force.

This breaking point with their true self is what is described in some traditions as "loss of paradise". The more they focus on imposing their truth by force, the more they will disintegrate and their reality will be distorted. The way in which they solve this is known in the Enneagram as mental fixation, and *Eights* begin to fixate on the need to get revenge on the world that stole their innocence.

"healthy view of the world".

Mental fixation: "I have to be strong to avoid getting hurt"

Eights impose their truth on others, and when they do not comply with their rules, punishment ensues. So, what is seen on the outside as revenge, *Eights* think of as justice. This need to be strong to impose their truth on others triggers the passion of *Eights*, which is lust. It is that insatiable need to have more and more control over situations and other people, to avoid getting hurt and to feel strong and invulnerable. Accepting their vulnerability is the only thing that will make them shed that disproportionate fear of being weak. The *Eight* child thinks: *"This world belongs to the strong, so I will avoid showing my vulnerability at any cost."*

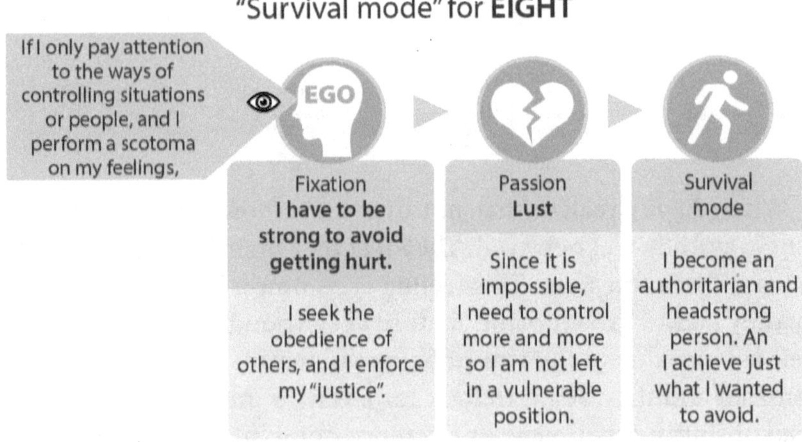

This strategy will manifest, as in all Enneatypes, through one of the three instincts, which in the case of *Eights* are:

- Preservation instinct: They seek control by satisfying all their physical needs.
- Social instinct: They seek power and social control.
- Sexual instinct: They seek to control those they care about.

How is the ego structure upheld?

Ego's mechanisms:

- Scotoma: Towards their vulnerability.
- Selective attention: Towards the weak spots of others in order to control them.
- Defense mechanism: Denial

Denial[67] is used by *Eights* to unconsciously negate something that makes them feel anxious by disavowing its very existence. These can include thoughts, feelings, wishes, sensations, needs, and other external factors that are unacceptable to the *Eight* for some reason. Denial comes in a variety of forms. A person may deny the reality of the unpleasant information altogether, admit that something is true but deny or minimize its seriousness, or admit that both the information and its severity are true but deny any personal responsibility for it. *Eights* exhibit denial on a regular basis, but they do so most blatantly when they feel anxious, vulnerable, sad, or intensely angry for long periods of time. Eventually, however, the denial stops working as they come face to face with a crisis they have been avoiding.

How do *Eights* think?

Basic fear
Of being vulnerable or controlled by someone.

Cognitive error
Eights are more assertive than other children, and produce stronger reactions in their parents, which they interpret as rejection. In response, *Eights* will seek independence and avoid weakness at all costs.

---

[67] Lapid-Bogda, G. (2019), Enneagram Learning portal. www.theenneagraminbusiness.com

Motivation

To gain power and control to make things happen.

Strategic skill of *Eights*

They skill they develop, according to Elaine De Beauport's[68] theory, is **basic intelligence**, which gives the human being the ability to approach and walk away properly from a given situation. It is the impulse to action. One of its special uses is to open up ways to explore new things.

> Basic intelligence means having access to our own life, being in charge of it and our billions of cells. It means being free to move the organism-mind-body-structure to get what we need. This also requires understanding that life is living itself in the configuration of a body we call "our own".
>
> The basic intelligence is there to provide the freedom of acting to maintain life itself. In the freedom to be, the practice of self-observation is key because it allows us to collect at the same time data from our body, such as our environment, our behavior and our dreams. This intelligence implies the search for balance with the whole. (p. 295)

The importance of self-observation in the control of these energy sources must be emphasized. It is precisely what *Eights* lack when they are not in high integration levels. They are visceral and explosive. They let this intelligence dominate and lead them to obtain what they want at any given moment without going through a process of reflexive analysis beforehand, which afterwards triggers conflict and inappropriate behaviors. In children, we may notice behaviors such as bullying, abuse of power or exclusion towards their classmates.

---

[68] Beauport, E. y Díaz, A. (2008), *Las tres caras de la mente. El desarrollo de las inteligencias mentales, emocionales y del comportamiento (The Three Faces of Mind: Developing Your Mental, Emotional, and Behavioral Intelligences)*, 1ª ed., Caracas, Venezuela: Alfa Grupo Editorial.

How to change the cognitive pattern of *Eight*

Eights avoid feeling their vulnerability at all costs, and, therefore, they exaggerate their basic intelligence in order to take whatever they desire. This can turn them into bullies. To deal with this issue, teachers usually ask the child to control their explosive character and their strength. They could not be more wrong, since these behaviors are generated as a defense to their feeling of vulnerability. The child has to be taught that it is all right to be vulnerable sometimes. Developing the **affective intelligence of the limbic brain,** which refers to the ability of letting oneself be affected by people, ideas, objects or expressions is recommended.

Tips to improve if you are an *Eight*

- Stop, reflect and digest information before making an impulsive decision.
- Learn to channel that great energy in a positive way: help, build, drive, instead of destroying, oppressing and controlling.
- Notice the positive and negative impact your energy has on others.
- Beware that behind your aggression, there is a lot of hidden fear that you don't want to recognize.
- Remember that someone who is sensitive and vulnerable is much STRONGER than someone who represses and denies their own emotions.
- Use your vitality and energy to leave a mark, a legacy that serves others.

Nine: The Harmonizer

Calm, conciliatory, adaptable, easy-going

Nines seek to keep inner and outer peace. They avoid conflict and judgment and are impartial most of the time. They simplify their problems and minimize anything that threatens their peace. Harmony is so important to them that they may take on the opinions and interests of others just to keep the peace. Routines and habits provide them with a sense of certainty, though they usually leave important tasks for later.

Characteristic behaviors

Automatic mode

Nines are good mediators, negotiators and advisors. They have great skill in handling people since they are calm, modest and simple. They are optimistic, emotionally stable, and they have a great sense of humor. They are calm and conformist pacifiers. They seek to keep inner and outer peace. They avoid conflict and almost always impartial judges. They forget themselves and their interest and opinions, replacing them with those of others. *"The other is more important than me."* They simplify their problems and minimize any situation that threatens their peace of mind. They let problems sort themselves out. They do not like change; and can be trapped in routines and habits that provide comfort. They leave important tasks for later and replace them with non-essential activities.

Survival mode

In more threatening circumstances, they are extremely apathetic, indecisive and stubborn. They are absent-minded and drowsy. They stick to others and they lose themselves to them. They have no identity and get depressed. They cannot confront reality, and lose themselves to food, drink, TV, etc.

Rational mode

They know what they want and where they are heading. They are profound and able to face any situation. They are in touch with their essence, and able to see themselves and feel important. Therefore, they will remain connected with their environment. They believe that the world is a loving place where we can all live in peace. The awareness of this love makes them move through life with deep compassion and an unmovable peace in their hearts. *"My attention will be on actively generating peace and harmony for the world."* Everything has a place in the world, and *Nines* know how to bestow it.

How ego is formed

When *Nines* separate from their essence, the environment ceases to be safe and nourishing and begins to be a threat to the child's safety. For this reason, *Nines* begin to perceive that their needs are not met. *"The world is a hostile place; I would like to go back to the womb, where everything was peace and quiet."* They start by not accepting reality, and begin to passively resist the world as it is, by not letting themselves be affected by their environment.

This child adapts to the hostile and minimally nurturing environment by being quiet. They draw the following conclusions: "My needs are not important." "If I cry, I get it worse." "It is useless to complain." "Do not be selfish." "Others should go before me."

Nines perceive that the environment does not pay attention to them, and that their needs are not satisfied when they arise but rather when their protective figure chooses. This makes *Nines* form an image of themselves as not deserving of attention and care, and their attention will be fixed on keeping a harmonious relationship with the environment so it takes care of them. Their vision or construction of the world will be the consequence of this way of looking at it.

Core construct: "This world does not value me, so it is pointless to make any effort"

Oscar Ichazo presented the concept of Holy Ideas, and *Nines*' is Holy Love[69]. The healthy view of *Nines* can be understood as the ability to see that we are all loved and important in this world. *Nines* have the natural quality of harmonizing environments and people, since they consider that everyone matters the same. When *Nines* apply their golden rule to themselves and become aware of the importance of their presence in this world, they become proactive and assertive. Nothing will give more peace to *Nines* than doing what they need to do at the proper time. The ability to see an aspect of reality without distortion or judgment is what I call healthy view, and, to my understanding, it is the equivalent to Ichazo's Holy Ideas.

In essence, *Nines* are able to perceive "Unconditional Love" in the world, and the virtue of Right Action arises in them, since they know their presence matters and they dare to take action.

"Rational Mode" for NINE

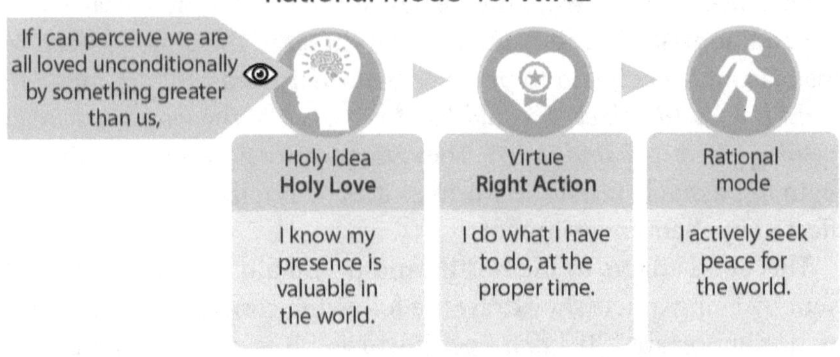

When *Nines* separate from their essence, they begin to look for ways to satisfy their need for connection. Instead of seeking that connection with themselves, they choose to connect to the exterior by reconciling and flowing with the environment. This breaking point with their true self is what is described in some traditions as "loss

---

[69] In the business world, these terms are not well received, that is why I call them "healthy view of the world".

of paradise". The more they focus on generating peace, the more they will disintegrate. The way in which they solve this is known in the Enneagram as mental fixation, and when *Nines* begin to detect an environment that does not look after them, their conclusion, from their child's perspective, is that they do not matter, so, why even try? It is easier not to make any noise, to go with the flow and adapt to be at peace. They learn that if others are fine, their chances of being taken care of will be greater, so they start harmonizing the environment as well. *Nines* draw the following conclusion: *"If I do not give any trouble, my mom will look after me at some point; I must just be patient."*

Mental fixation of Nines: "I have to be at peace and to generate harmony around me"

This fixation of looking for peace by putting others' needs ahead of their own makes *Nines* lose their personal power and motivation to do things, due to their feeling of little worth. Ichazo describes *Nines'* fixation as indolence, which I understand as the conviction that nothing they do matters, and thus, sloth emerges.

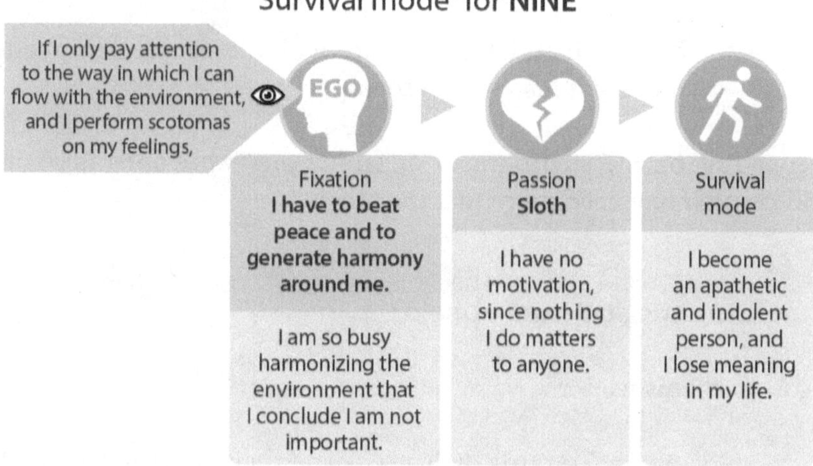

This passion is particularly misunderstood by mothers of teenagers who lie on a couch devouring junk food and TV. "When facing the loss of the feeling of being loved, I disconnect from the environment and I withdraw to an inner sanctuary, where I live in the safety of my imagination." Sloth is not overcome with reprimands or willpower. The only thing that eliminates sloth is motivation for life, which is a result of feeling noticed, and of knowing themselves to be important to those around them.

In the search for peace, *Nines* cut off any connection to their feelings of pain or need, and favor the perception of the environment in order to keep peace around them. My proposal is bold, and it requires further study, but after reviewing the chronic syndrome of insensitivity to pain, I dare say that *Nines* develop indifference towards their bodily perceptions as a way of survival. *Nines* know their needs will not be satisfied as they come up, so they have to take their own needs out of their attentional focus.

This strategy will manifest, as in all Enneatypes, through one of the three instincts, which in the case of *Nines* are:

- Preservation instinct: Being at peace with themselves, by becoming narcotized with TV, food or sleep.
- Social instinct: Generating peace for the world by working hard for others, with no thought for themselves or their needs.
- Sexual instinct: Being at peace with the people who matter to them and fusing with them.

Depending on the environment or family they were born into, they will develop one need more that the other.

How is the ego structure upheld?

Ego's mechanisms:

- Scotoma: Towards their needs and their anger for not being noticed.

- Selective attention: Towards the needs and angry reactions of others to be able to please them.
- Defense mechanism: Narcotization

Narcotization[70] is a psychological defense mechanism in which *Nines* unconsciously numb themselves to avoid something that feels too large, complex, difficult, or uncomfortable to handle. They narcotize and distract themselves by engaging in prolonged rhythmic activities that are familiar, require very little attention, and provide comfort – for example, washing the dishes, working in the garden, continuous pleasure reading of books by the same author or within the same genre, going for a walk or a bike ride, engaging in frequent or extended casual conversations, or continuously changing channels on television. *Nines* also use daily routines such as morning or evening rituals to immunize themselves from being fully aware, and they feel agitated, irritated, or disoriented when these repetitive activities become disrupted.

Most *Nines* engage in narcotizing activities on a regular basis, but they do this most often when they feel pressured, uncertain, angry, anxious about their ability to do something, discounted or overlooked, and more. It can be difficult to determine what is upsetting *Nines*, because even they may not know for certain. However, when they engage in narcotizing behavior – especially when there is something else they should be doing or something they need to say – it is a clear indication that they have deadened themselves with something distracting and soothing.

How do *Nines* think?

Basic fear
To lose connection and peace.

Cognitive error

---

[70] Lapid-Bogda, G. (2019), Enneagram Learning portal. www.theenneagraminbusiness.com

Nines believe that their needs are not important for others, and therefore they must wait for the environment to take care of them when it decides to, which leads them to generate an anger that they repress and disconnection from themselves.

Motivation
Achieving peace and harmony.

Strategic skill of *Nines*

The ability *Nines* develop, according to Elaine De Beauport's[71] theory, is **pattern intelligence**.

> *The pattern which entails the organization of energy in the reptilian brain has a stabilizing or harmonizing function, from where it would be possible to suppose that resistance to change comes from.*
>
> *Pattern intelligence is the one that enables us to store the experiences between stimulus and response which were functional at a given moment in our life. These stimuli triggered responses in us, which formed patterns, which, in turn, are used to filter all the information we get throughout our life. Our patterns were incorporated to our life when we were children; hence, those experiences determine us as time passes by. "Patterns are the way in which experiences happen first; memory is the register of patterns so that they continue to be available". (p. 325)*

Actually, nowadays we know these patterns as somatic markers. Once they are formed, they can be stimulated in many ways and sometimes they will make us feel uncomfortable, without us even being aware of what pattern triggered that discomfort. *Nines* learned to live ruled by those patterns, and to not to leave them. That is why they respond in an

---

[71] Beauport, E. y Díaz, A. (2008), *Las tres caras de la mente. El desarrollo de las inteligencias mentales, emocionales y del comportamiento (The Three Faces of Mind: Developing Your Mental, Emotional, and Behavioral Intelligences)*, 1ª ed., Caracas, Venezuela: Alfa Grupo Editorial.

automatic manner to all of the environment's stimuli without asking themselves what they truly want.

Understanding which patterns guide us, and how these patters stabilize our subtle energy, allows us to delve into them until we discover their origin, in order to intervene and modify them to achieve greater well-being.

The ego will automatically activate response patterns, and if they do not become aware of their existence, *Nines* will become automatons that react to external stimuli without mediating any analysis of their emotions or desires. Claudio Naranjo describes the disintegrated *Nines* as a people with elephant skin, who are numb to all their perceptions and who chose to favor external stimuli over their own to achieve harmony with the environment. Giving up their illusions and desires brings about a perfect adaptation to the environment, but it produces the indolence that is so typical of *Nines*. In other words: *"If I gave up my needs for the sake of harmony, do not ask me to care about yours."* This is how *Nines* disconnect more and more from the world to live in permanent apathy before any event.

Automatic response patterns hinder freedom of action. A conscious observation of these patterns enables *Nines* to analyze them and modify the inappropriate ones, thus being able to embrace their own needs from an updated reality.

Since this ability to act in accordance to established patterns provides safety to *Nines*, the more threatened they feel, the more they will adjust their responses to previously established patterns. As they go down the integration levels, they seek to feel at peace and in harmony with the environment, even if that means giving up on their own aspirations and desires. As the awareness level decreases, there will be a greater scotoma towards their inner perception, and a greater attention towards the outside world in order to harmonize it.

How to change the cognitive pattern of *Nines*

The only way to modify Nine's patterns is through a conscious analysis of their effectiveness. That is, they have to analyze their origin and function, to decide whether they remain operative or not. Let us remember that the brain will always pick what it deems more adequate for survival, so it will be necessary to change *Nines'* belief that they do not matter. Once they have done this, they will modify their behavior and will cease to act in accordance to automatic patterns, to use their neocortex and respond consciously to external stimuli.

Another highly useful thing for *Nines* is to realize that a small conflict may spare them many later conflicts. Being assertive brings more peace than saying yes to everything and not following through afterwards.

When *Nines* realize doing things in time brings about more peace that procrastinating, they will intuitively become more organized.

Tips to improve if you are a *Nine*

- Set goals, structure yourself, do not waste time on trivial things and finish what you start.
- Learn to set limits, to say NO, to be more assertive and less complacent and flattering.
- Dare to face and make small decisions. The more you avoid having conflicts, the more problems you will have.
- Do not postpone the decisions you can make; Your people and customers need answers, not just good intentions.
- Express and defend your goals and your opinion directly and concretely, without devaluing them through humor; and seriously commit yourself to acting.

Conclusions

My conclusion is that the Ego, or personality, is the result of an adaptive process of the human being which begins during gestation and that models the brain in order to attain the highest efficiency possible. Taking into account that the brain is like the whole human being, an unfinished organ that transforms and adapts to the needs of the individual that it serves, we are able to transform it to the extent that we dare to question our paradigms and reference constructs.

Since I started studying the Enneagram, I have heard people say that personality is the lens through which we filter everything that happens to us, and I take great pleasure in being able to explain how this process takes place from the neurocognitive point of view.

A big difference between the Enneagram and other theories used in organizations is that the Enneagram not only talks about behaviors, but motivations and beliefs as well. It does not tell us what to do; rather it explains why we do what we do and helps us understand why it is so difficult to change. I always tell my students that, in order to transform yourself, you do not have to do more things, but you have to stop doing the things you always do automatically. It seems to be that perception is the origin of our behavior, and it is precisely our perception that we must transform if we wish to transform ourselves.

Picking up where we left off with neuroscientific facts in the first chapter, and remembering that nature seeks the survival of the species by keeping us in a safe zone, we will only be able to change as we consciously design a new survival strategy that our brain considers to be more useful.

The Enneagram helps us discover the story our brain has told us throughout out life, in order to modify it and to have a better perception of reality, which will give us the skill to respond in a more adequate manner to our current situation, instead of continuing to react from our own personal history.

As we get to know ourselves more, we understand the environment better. This only happens when we allow ourselves to question the frame of reality that had worked for us so far. The Enneagram is a great tool because it enables the human being to review their egoic conducts, without threatening their true essence. Helping people to feel comfortable analyzing their actions is possible from the perspective of knowing that WE ARE NOT OUR BEHAVIORS. That is why, as I delve into the Enneagram and share it with more people, I notice its kindness brings about great changes, because they do not feel threatened when reviewing their past, and they know that the more they do it, the closer they will be to their true essence. To know that within us there is something that is presence, light, love, or image and likeness of God, is encouraging. The only thing we have to do, **is to stop doing what we have been doing to start BEING what we already are from the moment we were created.**

The Enneagram proves that each personality thinks very differently, and that is why it helps people understand and make their mindset more flexible, to transform it into a "Learning Mindset". The brain realizes its possibilities of survival radically increase if it learns new things and accepts different people.

The Enneagram helps transform our deepest beliefs, update our frames of reference, and remodel our brain structures. This increases the ability to perceive reality in a less distorted manner. People lose less control of themselves and their life begins to improve in every way; they begin to detect opportunities instead of looking out for threats. This is what Daniel Goleman called emotional intelligence.

Another kindness of the Enneagram is that it generates awareness, and, therefore, the person is able to take charge of their life. The word "responsibility" implies the ability to respond in a different way, and that will only be accomplished through awareness. Disintegrated people attack and threaten society because they are disabled by their own mental processes, unable to realize that their behaviors have not been functional. That is why I firmly believe it is not about regulating human beings' behavior with more laws and punishment, rather it is about giving back to people the dignity of their essence through mechanisms that make them responsible for their life, so they can be the generators of their own change.

If we use the nine patterns or mental constructs the Enneagram proposes, we will see that they make sense out of the cognitive-behavioral patterns shown by people. In the same way, we will look at the reticular activating system (ARAS) and scotomas as mechanisms that aid survival, and not as mere interference in learning. The way in which certain types of *stimulus* are favored and what memories are stored, has to do with the conformation that was more useful during our first childhood; they are not topics of chance. If we understand that synaptic pruning processes have a certain logic, and that, by making ourselves aware of these patterns we can modify them, synaptic paths leading to an integrated brain will appear naturally.

Even my observation over the years allows me to predict that the much-longed-for *perfect fit* that positive psychology mentions, may be attained by getting to know the nine constructs of the Enneagram.

If you are thinking of starting the study of the Enneagram, do not believe anything I say; I invite you to research the widest possible range of teachers and theories. Keep what is useful for you and discard what has no bearing on your life.

Finally, I wish to invite all the Enneagram teachers to remember that, just as personalities are different views of reality, the Enneagram's theories are different paths that lead us to a common goal: self-knowledge and full understanding of the human being. I encourage all experts to stop fighting over the authorship of this or that concept, and instead, to work together for the sake of an integrated theory of the Enneagram. There are not better and worse views; they are all appreciations that contribute to and facilitate the coming together of people. Personally, some day, I wish to see this integrated theory of the Enneagram, which is the result of the sum of all valuable concepts, and where all points of view fit in. How can we aspire to transform the world through this tool, if we are not even capable of transforming our small community? To wrap up, I want to share with you an idea I once heard from a great philosopher and friend:

"We are all born with a musical instrument, which is our essence. Our task is to find out what our instrument is, and to tune it to be able to play harmoniously in this orchestra that is life."

Roberto Pérez

Bibliographic references

1. Amthor, F. (2016) *Neuroscience for Dummies.* 2nd. ed. New Jersey: Ed. For Dummies.
2. Babatz, C. (2011). *Místico sin monasterio: manual de meditación y oración de contemplación.* México: Universidad Iberoamericana.
3. Beauport, E. y Díaz, A. (2008) *Las tres caras de la mente. El desarrollo de las inteligencias mentales, emocionales y del comportamiento.* 1st. Ed., Caracas, Venezuela: Alfa Grupo Editorial
4. Belmonte, Carlos. (2014) *El dolor, ¿mecanismo de defensa o castigo?* Transcripción de la conferencia dictada en la decimoséptima edición del Programa de Promoción de la Cultura Científica y Tecnológica, organizado por la Real Academia de Ciencias Exactas, Físicas y Naturales.
5. Bouyer, L. (1978). *History of Christian Spirituality, The Spirituality of The New Testament and the Fathers.* New York: The Seabury Press.
6. Carey, N. (2013). *La revolución epigenética.* 1st. Ed. España: Ediciones de Intervención Cultural.
7. Carter, R. (2014). *The Human Brain Book.* 2nd. ed. New York: DK.
8. Damásio, A.(2011) *El error de Descartes.* 1st. ed. Barcelona: Editorial Andrés Bello.
9. De Jesús, T. (2016). *El libro de las moradas.* 1st. ed. España: e-Book Classic Alba.
10. Empereur, J. (2000) *El Eneagrama y la dirección espiritual.* Nueve caminos para la guía espiritual. 1st. ed. Barcelona: Ed. Desclée.
11. Fauvre, K. (2017) *Enneagram Instinctual Subtypes.* Edición revisada. Estados Unidos: Selfpublished.
12. Fernández, F. (2016) ¿De dónde demonios salió el Eneagrama? 1st. ed. México: Ed Pax.
13. Frade, L. (2011) *Diseño de situaciones didácticas.* México. D.F.: Calidad Educativa.

14. Gautier, R. y Boeree, G. (2006). *Teorías de la Personalidad: una selección de los mejores autores del siglo XX*. Santo Domingo: Editorial UNIBE.

15. Goleman, D. (2014). *EL punto ciego, psicología del autoengaño*. 4th. Ed., México: Editorial Me gusta leer.

16. Guitton, J. (1996) *El genio de Teresa de Lisieux*. Madrid: EDICEP.

17. González, C. (2003). *Bésame mucho.* España: Diseño Editorial, S.L. Retrieved from: <http://potencialgestante.com.br/wp-content/uploads/2014/01/Carlos-Gonz%C3%A1les-Besame-Mucho.pdf>. [Consulted: april 10, 2015].

18. González, M.V.C. (2011). Estilos de aprendizaje: su influencia para aprender a aprender. *Revista Estilos de Aprendizaje*, 7(7). Retrieved from: <http://www2.uned.es/revistaestilosdeaprendizaje/numero_7/articulos/lsr_7_articulo_12.pdf> [Consulted: december 14, 2016].

19. González, J. y Rubio, J. (2013). *Evagrio Póntico. Obras espirituales*. Madrid: Ed. Ciudad Nueva.

20. Kofman, F. (2008). *La empresa consciente*. 1st. ed. Buenos Aires, Argentina: Editorial Aguilar.

21. Lapid-Bogda, G. (2006). *Eneagrama y éxito personal.* 1st. ed. España: Editorial Urano.

22. Lapid-Bogda, G. (2018). *The Art of Typing.* 1st. ed. Santa Mónica, USA: The Enneagram in Business Press.

23. Lipton, B. (2007). *La biología de la creencia*. 1st. Ed., Madrid: Editorial Palmyra.

24. Llull, R. *Ars Brevis*. (1432). Palma de Mallorca: Manuscrito. Retrieved from: <http://bvpb.mcu.es/es/consulta/resultados_busqueda.cmd?posicion=1&forma=ficha&id=31>. [Consulted: september 28, 2015].

25. Maitri, S. (2005). *The Enneagram of Passions and Virtues.* 1st. ed. New York: Penguin Group.

26. Murphy, A. (2010). *Origins: How the Nine Months Before Birth Shape the Rest of Our Lives.* 1st. Ed. New York: Free Press.

27. Naranjo, C. (2012) *Carácter y Neurosis*. 11th. ed. Barcelona: Ed. La Llave.

28. Nieto, J. (2011). *Neurodidáctica: Aportaciones de las neurociencias al aprendizaje y la enseñanza*. Madrid: Editorial CCS.

29. Palmer, H. Y Brown, P (1997). *The Enneagram Advantage.* 1st. ed. USA: Random House.

30. Portellano, J.A. (2008) *Introducción a la Neuropsicología.* 1st. ed., Madrid: McGraw-Hill Education.

31. Pierce, K. B. (2014) *La Escalera Espiritual de San Pedro.* Lima: Fondo Editorial.

32. Riso, R. y Husdon, R (1996). *Personality Types.* 1st. Ed. USA: Houghton Miffln Company.

33. Riso, H. y Hudson, R (2000). *La sabiduría del Eneagrama.* 1st. Ed. Barcelona, España: Ediciones Urano, S. A.

34. Riso, H. y Hudson, R (2000). *Understanding the Enneagram.* Revised Ed. USA: Houghton Mifflin Company.

35. Schultz, D. y Schultz, S. (2002). *Teorías de la Personalidad.* 7th. Ed. México: Thomson.

36. Sikora, M. y Tallon, R. (2012). *Conciencia en acción.* 1st. wd. España: Editorial Gullab.

37. Spidlik, T. (1986) *The Spirituality of the Christian East.* A *sistematic handbook.* Kalamazoo, USA: Cistercian Publications.

38. Siegel, D. And Hartzell, M. *(2014) Parenting from the Inside Out:* How a Deeper Self-Understanding Can Help You Raise Children Who Thrive. 10th aniv. ed. London: Scribe Publications.

39. Siegel, D. y Payne,T. (2012). *El cerebro del niño.* 1st. ed. Barcelona: Alba Editorial.

40. Vargas, A. (2016) *El Eneagrama.* ¿Quién soy? Nueva Ed. México: Alamah.

41. Wagner, J. (2010). Nine Lenses of the World. 1st. ed. Evanston, Illinois: Nine Lens Press.

42. Webster, M. (2016). *Merrian-Webster Dictionary.* Springfield: Merrian-Webster Inc.

43. Wilber, Ken. (1988) *El ojo del Espíritu.* España: Ed. Kairós.

Agustina Burgos article references

1. Beauport, E. y Díaz, A. (2008). Las tres caras de la mente. El desarrollo de las inteligencias mentales, emocionales y del comportamiento. 1st. Ed., Caracas, Venezuela: Alfa Grupo Editorial

2. Goleman, D. (1996). The Three Faces of Mind. Developing your Mental, Emotional and Behavioral Intelligences . Wheatox, Illinois: Editorial Quest Books.

3. Goleman, D. (2000). *Emotional Intelligence.* Nueva York: Bantam Books.

4. Rosenzweig, M. y Leiman, A. (2002). *Psicología Fisiológica.* Editorial McGraw-Hill Education.

5. Nicol, M. (1973). *Comentarios psicológicos sobre las enseñanzas de Gurdjieff y Ouspensky.* Ed. Kier.

6. Teilhard de Chardin, P. *El Porvenir del Hombre.* España: Ed. Taurus.

Magazines

1. Aboitiz, F. Y Schöter, C. (2005). Síndrome de Déficit de Atención: Antecedentes Neurobiológicos y cognitivos para estudiar un modelo de endofenotipo. *Revista chilena de neuro-psiquiatría.* 43(1):11-16. Retrieved from: <http://www.scielo.cl/scielo.php?script=sci_arttext&pid=S0717-92272005000100002&lng=es&nrm=iso>. [Consulted: december 12, 2016].

2. Ávila, G. (2005). *Diferencias en los Estilos de Apego entre Niños con Padres Casados y Divorciados.* (Tesis para obtener el grado de licenciatura en Psicología). Universidad de las Américas. Puebla, Cholula. Retrieved from: <http://catarina.udlap.mx/u_dl_a/tales/documentos/lps/avila_a_gv/>. [Consulted: december 17, 2016].

3. Castaingts, J. (2008). *Antropología simbólica y neurociencia. Revista Alteridades.* 18(35). Retrieved from: <http://www.scielo.org.mx/scielo.php?script=sci_arttext&pid=S0188-70172008000100010>.

4. *Enfoques de aprendizaje y dominancias cerebrales entre estudiantes universitarios.* (2004). Retrieved from: <https://dialnet.unirioja.es/servlet/articulo?codigo=1307814>. [Consulted: december 17, 2016].

5. Gómez-Pérez, E., Ostrosky-Solís, F., Próspero-García, O. (2003). Desarrollo de la atención, la memoria y los procesos inhibitorios: relación temporal con la maduración de la estructura y función cerebral, *Revista de Neurología,* 37(6):561-567. Retrieved from: <https://www.neurologia.com/revista/37/06>. [Consulted: june 2, 2017].

6. Nardi, D. (2013). Neurociencia y Eneagrama. *Revista "N"*. 1(2):13-18. Retrieved from: <http://www.aeneagrama.es/>. [Consulted: december 5, 2016].

7. Nardi, D. (2012). Neuroscience meet the Enneagram. *Nine Points Magazine.*International Enneagram Association Jul-Sep, 10-16. USA. Retrieved from: <http://www.ninepointsmagazine.org/articles/>. [Consulted: december 26, 2016 and the author].

8. Newgent, R.A., Parr, P.E., Newman, I. and Higgins, K.K. (2004). *The Riso-Hudson Enneagram type indicator: estimates of reliability measurement and evaluation.* 1st. Ed. Estados Unidos: Enneagram Journal.

9. Redes atencionales y sistema visual selectivo. (2006). Retrieved from: <http://www.scielo.org.co/scielo.php?script=sci_arttext&pid=S1657-92672006000200009>. [Consulted: september 28, 2016].

10. Valderrama, H. R. (2006). La teoría de Karen Horney. *Revista Psicologia.com,* 10(1):15-17. México: BUAP. Retrieved from: <http://www.psiquiatria.com/revistas/index.php/psicologiacom/article/viewFile/746/721/>. [Consulted: december 10, 2016].

Blogs

1. Alva, M. (2005, marzo). Orígenes de la palabra personalidad. *Revista avances en salud.* Retrieved from: <http://manuelalvaolivos.obolog.es/origenes-palabra-personalidad-60660>. [Consulted: january 3, 2017].

2. Salazar, C. (2010, 11 de diciembre). *Hamarteología.* Retrieved from: <https://csalazar.org/2010/12/11/hamarteologa/>. [Consulted: january 2, 2016].

Videos

1. Lipton (2015) ¿El Por qué Enfermamos? Retrieved from: <https://www.youtube.com/watch?v=YZHFg1zo4zA> [Consulted: december 13, 2017].

2. Bergman, N. (2013) *Restaurando el paradigma original.* Retrieved from: <https://www.youtube.com/watch?v=Kb_4DSrmdZQ>. [Consulted: november 20, 2017].

3. Siegel (2012) *Presenting a Hand Model of the Brain.* Retrieved from: <https://www.youtube.com/watch?v=gm9CIJ74Oxw>. [Consulted: january 10, 2017].

About de author

International speaker, corporate consultant, coach and IEA-accredited teacher of the Enneagram, **Adelaida Harrison** holds a Masters degree in Cognitive Neuroscience and Learning. She has studied with leading Enneagram teachers around the world including Don Riso, Russ Hudson, David Daniels, Ginger Lapid Bogda and Roberto Pérez, among others.

Co-founder of the first Enneagram school in Latin America accredited by the International Ennneagram Association, she is a Senior Member of Enneagram in Business Network, the largest network of business Enneagram consultants in the world.

Together with Andrea Vargas, she has presented a weekly radio program on MVS Mexico City dedicated to the Enneagram since 2012. Her radio show regularly attracts an audience of over 150 000 people who are eager to learn how the Enneagram can help them achieve their potential.